Landscape
of the Heart

WRITINGS ON DAUGHTERS AND JOURNEYS

STEPHEN J. LYONS

WSU PRESS

Washington State University Press
Pullman, WA 99164-5910

Washington State University Press, Pullman, Washington 99164-5910
©1996 by the Board of Regents of Washington State University
All rights reserved
First printing 1996

Many of the essays in this book appeared in different forms in *Northern Lights, Manoa, Idaho the University, The Bloomsbury Review, High Country News, The Sun,* and *Utne Reader.* An excerpt of "Moving Through the Landscape of Healing" appeared in the book, *In Black and White: Idaho Photography and Writing* (Prichard Gallery/Confluence Press, 1994), and a portion of "Driving Alone" was published in the calendar, *Palouse Expressions.*

Poems in the book were published in *Spoon River Poetry Review, Witness, The Redneck Review of Literature, Kinesis, High Country News, Grain,* and *Poem.*

Library of Congress Cataloging-in-Publication Data
Lyons, Stephen J.
    Landscape of the heart : writings on daughters and journeys /
Stephen J. Lyons.
        p.   cm.
    ISBN 0-87422-132-3.—ISBN 0-87422-133-1 (pbk.)
    1. Fathers and daughters—United States—Poetry.   2. Poets, American—20th century—Family relationships.   3. Lyons, Stephen J.—
Family.   I. Title.
PS3562.Y44945L3   1966   95-26672
818' .5409—dc20   CIP

Washington State University Press
Pullman, Washington 99164-5910
Phone: (800) 354-7360
Fax: (509) 335-8568

Landscape
of the Heart

For Rose

CONTENTS

"Stephen, as I wrote in a poem once:
'not to be dead to each other'—
that being the main striving—
though we're tested severely,
our talking about that,
the job of rebuilding from loss,
trusting into the next good."

—note from Tess Gallagher
February 23, 1989

Preface

O N JULY 24, 1980, the eve of my daughter's birth in rural
northern Michigan, I made the following entries in my
journal: "Contractions starting at 11:30 p.m., five minutes apart lasting thirty seconds, centered toward Shari's lower
back. Spent the day with morning milking chores at barn, home
for forty-five minutes, feeling impatient, torn between summer
field work and events at home. Five and a half hours cultivating
the north barley field, back to the home farm for the evening
milking, then racing the mile home. Our mid-wife Tai and her
assistant Nedra arrive. Good, clear talk as we sat together on the
floor gathered around Shari for support. A light supper of miso
soup, crackers, juice, and tea. After the meal Shari and I walk up
the road to the edge of the birch forest feeling very close and connected by the impending life. Fireflies snap in the heavy air of
humidity. We feel that our daughter is already with us."

When Meghan Rose Lyons came into the world the next
morning at 8:30 a light rain began, the gentlest of showers usually associated with spring, not the dramatic mid-summer thunderstorms of the upper peninsula we'd been experiencing. Her
home-birth arrival was also peaceful—no spanking to test the
vocal cords, no useless chemicals dropped into her dark eyes, no
routine episiotomy, no washing away of the sweet vernix, no interference. All of us marveled at the good fortune of the rain, the
joining of sky to earth, the fertility of water reaching through the

dark Midwest soil and nourishing the large prehistoric lakes moving beneath the futon in the tiny room where Rose was born. We could hear the vague, familiar voices of men working in the distance, moving the second cutting of hay from the wagons to the barn behind the house. Light raindrops and the rich smell of cut alfalfa intertwined with the fragrance of birth. Through the bedroom window I knew the pear tree was sagging with the burden of another form of life. Mint grew along the front porch. Asparagus waved tall in the ditches, signaling for our attention. Apples were already forming in the orchard. Sixty green, beefsteak tomato plants rose above the choking hold of quack grass in our garden where we would eventually bury the placenta. All around us was the sensuality of life. That morning I took it all inside, felt every fibrous stalk, every drop of moisture, every nuance of shade and spray. It was one of those rare moments usually only entered by yogis and Buddhist zazen masters where one is exactly in the present tense, where you can feel the earth turning out from its core, and you are at the center, on the verge of everything all at the same time.

From the moment I caught my daughter and cut the life cord from her mother, my life changed forever. It was my birth as well and the cord to my past was severed. Rose came into this life to enhance an ongoing connection between my interior and exterior landscapes. And I knew we would explore this together. Father and daughter. Best friends. On that July day I also knew I wanted to take her to many places: to the canyons and mesas of the Southwest desert; to the red rocks and river cottonwoods in autumn splendor; and to the urban landscapes of my own youth. And I wanted to show her Yellowstone most of all.

I would get my opportunity sooner than expected. A month after Rose arrived we were told we no longer would have jobs at the dairy and we would have to leave our pastoral home. The self-inflicted farm crisis of the 1970s finally caught us, in the northernmost stretches of the Midwest. Hired hands like us were expendable. And vulnerable. Our boss said he was "sorry, of course . . . you know with the baby being so young . . . with winter coming on . . . nothing personal . . . but we can't afford . . . and, by the way, before you move out, paint the house. I'll bring the brushes around in the morning."

I remember receiving the news out by the garden while listening to Shari sing remnants from madrigals and Bach cantatas as she vacuumed the back porch. I could see her figure moving gracefully as I looked past the owner toward my little family. Her beautiful alto voice forever became the background music to another life change. Rose, wearing a blue bonnet, was shaded under the apple trees in a car seat guarded by my blue heeler, Emmie Lou Lyons. Where would we go?

Later, in October, with our home in a few boxes, I stood in the middle of the garden and with the slow deliberation of a psychopath, I hurled my anger against the fates by pelting the heifers, the bull, and the two steers with ripe tomatoes. I am not ashamed of my rage. I let my dark, male side be my guide for once. I wanted red seeds splashed against the dull Holsteins; I wanted my hurt to take root in the dark, Michigan dirt. My green eyes flared with vengeance. When I finished I turned back to the house and saw the first flock of Canada geese overhead on their way south, as we would be soon. I would see them everywhere as we made our way back to the West. And they have followed me to this very day, always verifying the instability of life, always offering a way out.

Nine years later, almost to the day, after breaking each and every one of our wedding vows, Shari and I would be divorced.

This book is not about divorce. Or blame. What brings couples together can also pull them apart. It's the other side of magnets, the side that repels rather than attracts. We must play the cards we are dealt if we are to continue. If I have learned anything in my thirty-nine years it is that before forgiveness of others takes place, forgiveness of yourself must come first.

I've learned the first step toward that healing is a movement toward nature: revealed in the broken drumming of the woodpeckers and flickers, the rush of snow melt across basalt, the power and lure of mountain silver, the sound of the breeze in those great wind catchers—the cottonwoods—the redemption of another spring. Redemption for all of us. I've known this all my life but it took a daughter to remind me.

This book then is about loss, resurfacing, the ultimate healing that takes place on the American landscape, and how that landscape has been forever changed. The word benediction is usually associated with religious formalities (Are there two more beautiful words than redemption and benediction?), but benediction for my daughter and me has always taken place on the landscape, whether in the cool, ancient shadows of the coastal redwoods searching for banana slugs, in the pock-marked glacial lake country of eastern Washington coming upon two hundred trumpeter swans, on wind-swept Steens Mountain in the desert country of eastern Oregon, and on the cacophonous streets of Brooklyn, New York.

Rose has been there every step of the way.

Nor is this book about the differences of gender. There are enough books already written that isolate the sexes from each other. Yes, women and men can be at odds, but there are commonalties in the way we raise our children, the way we raise and nurture ourselves, and in the ways we approach solitude, despair, and finally, if we are fortunate, how we attempt a return to hope. I want this book to be a bridge from parents to children, fathers to mothers, and men to women. We need each other more than ever.

Rose and I have created original traditions and rituals that reflect our new family structure for five years now. This book is about those years. At times I have felt the weariness of a pioneer in the 1990s frontier of single-parenting, relying on my instincts instead of societal and family role models. After all, America remains stubbornly fixated with the idea of a "nuclear family" although it rarely exists anymore. Holidays are still geared toward that ideal, and being in your thirties, single, with a child is a wilderness experience. With that in mind, I especially want to dedicate these chapters as solace for all configurations of families whether there are children present or not. I don't believe that single-parent families are broken families. I don't believe that women and men need to have children to be complete. Quite to the contrary, I believe wherever there is love there is always family.

I see children as mirrors to our own selfishness. They have come into our lives to teach us how to live. They belong to all of us. Each one is hopeful and brave. It is time we listened to them.

Letter to Rose:
What Passes Through Our Hands

At the age of four months my grandfather held you, cradled in his cracked fingers, scarred forever by grease and failed farms. Around Cedar Rapids, Iowa, where men are defined by their jobs, they called him *Chuck from the bus garage*, the crazy Bohemian with his homemade berry wine, and sauerkraut fermenting in ancient wooden cylinders in the garage. Old Chuck, my mother's bilingual father, who only finished sixth grade and as far as I know never read a book or wrote anything down but his name on the back of a paycheck. My grandfather the dumpster diver from the Great Depression who retrieved every scrap of everything Iowa ever threw away and brought it all home.

On that deceivingly clear day in November, when the bright sun means bitter cold, a calm surrounds both of you, two generations and sixty years apart. In the distance, central Iowa with its perfect furrows of tasseled agribusiness and under-appreciated hills of humidity; its water towers painted with the names of small towns and high school graduates; and its WPA windbreaks and shiny silos filled with corn gas. Iowa, shaped like a pig, jumping off point to the Great Plains and the Rockies, surrounded on two sides by two of America's great blue-collar, working rivers—the Missouri and the Mississippi.

Corn and beans, pigs and polkas. Scattered pieces of walnut forests where my bare-footed grandmother Georgia gathered mushrooms in her floral apron, speaking all the time in Czech to herself, to my brother and me, to her three daughters, to her dead relatives. And probably to you, Rose. How I wish I'd listened more closely.

My grandmother died in 1982, along with the family history. On that same November day when you were handed over to her, Georgia Uchytil retold the family's stories to me again. But I was young, preoccupied with unemployment and a continuing uncertain future, between jobs and a home, and coming to the realization that having a daughter afforded a smaller margin of error than I'd been used to. Simply put, I didn't know the value of her stories. I wrote nothing down that afternoon and I will carry that regret with me to my own grave.

I sat in her kitchen kingdom for hours while she told story after story, as if she knew this would be her last chance and perhaps an anecdote or two might pass through a sieve to you. She rocked you, with the confidence that only a grandmother has, her heart pressed against your sleeping head. On her wall hung a calendar with the few personal words she allowed herself to write each day between the unending chores. Weather words and news of the season. *10 below and cold. Rained all day. Pick up dill and pears from Kremedy. Canned beans. Tornado in Keystone.* Routine structured the architecture of her life bordered by two flower gardens and a vegetable patch, the subsequent canning and freezing, rabbits and chickens on the side, and the saving and mostly doing without.

For more than thirty years, Grandpa left for the city garage each morning at around 4:00 in the morning to repair and paint buses. The *Cedar Rapids Gazette* came at 3:00 in the afternoon, followed by Grandpa, his green-visored, 1951 Chevy truck growling to a stop in the long driveway. In between, Georgia and Chuck ate their watermelon with salt; their tomatoes with sugar. At noon, the sirens announced the middle of the day from fire station to fire station. Train whistles blew on the trestles above the Cedar River where pools of catfish rested. Tornado warnings interrupted the all-night radio shows Grandma loved. Corn was shucked. Peas scooped out with thumbs to fall into silver bowls. Beans snapped in half. Grandkids were spoiled.

My grandmother firmly believed her own saying, "There's a place for everything and everything in its place." They hid silver dollars in flashlights; kept chenille on the bed and shotguns in the broom closet. Once, on her birthday in the middle of her morning chores, she heard Ray Charles singing "Georgia On My Mind" on the radio and she was convinced that he was singing each word just for her.

Grandma told me they always had enough to eat, even during the worst of the Depression; she remembered how they were relentlessly resented by the neighbors for their good luck and hard work. (To this day nothing is wasted by my grandfather, who still readies himself against the next Depression. The large stand-up freezer is packed to gills with every conceivable food item and he's never known a supermarket dumpster he hasn't liked.)

Together they worked hard to raise three daughters and in subtle ways to raise all of us who followed in their wake. They never called in sick, refused work, or turned away from acts of charity. I don't want to leave you with the impression that they were perfect, but I want you to know what was good about them.

I possess nothing of my grandparents. No oak furniture, ancient crumbling letters, a favored fishing pole, or pocket knife. What I can pass on to you are these images and stories. History, especially a family's, is elusive, and memory is, as it is often said, a poor guide. Hard work to write it down exactly right, although I've attempted to do just that. History is made in what appears to be at first glance mundane and ordinary ways. It's written at kitchen tables and printed in the small boxes of calendar days and in the opening and closing of lunch pails at noon. Sometimes in life it may seem as if nothing of consequence ever happens except the small acts of routine that occupy countless hours and ultimately frame our short lives. But I want you to know: *Everything counts.*

Pay attention to the subtle, to the seemingly inconsequential. Look at your own hands, the blood that runs through their veins, and remember where you come from: strong arms holding you with unconditional love. The feeling that you could never, ever fall.

First Summer, Running

"We've got to go if we're going,"
Sylvie said. "Are you all buttoned
up? You should have a hat." She
put her arm around my shoulder
and squeezed me. She whispered,
"It's not the worse thing, Ruthie,
drifting. You'll see. You'll see."

Marilynne Robinson
From *Housekeeping*

WE WERE FIERCE in our hurt, and coarse, like the desert sand that settled in our matted hair. We used our fingers as spoons, our shirts for thin pillows. We avoided main highways and, instead, stuck to washboard and gravel. We mocked the threat of bears in the Strawberry Mountains of Oregon and ate our apple butter-honey sandwiches without fear, left sugary offerings of crusts to sows and cubs. Death never entered our thoughts.

No destination, no time, no maps. We were running for all we were worth. We cared only about birds and the places they went. When the wind blew it called us by our names: Stephen and Rose; father and daughter. Rose sang barely beyond carshot. Sometimes I gave nothing back.

Don't tell me emotional hurt diminishes with time; that a broken heart mends. Save the speeches about pain being the great teacher. Running is what feels good. If you keep moving, the air rushes against your face and sculpts tiny lines of maps around your eyes. Places you'll want to visit. One step then another. Keep moving on grassy paths until you forget you are walking. Keep trusting in trees and clouds.

Say you were held under water long beyond the point of sustaining life. Above you the blue sky floated. But you didn't die. Instead you broke surface but still couldn't breathe. Water sticks to you, gives you weight, holds you back. Water. Air. Liquidity. Each is the reverse of the other. You need all to survive. Lose any one and you die.

We were motherless, lover-less, no wife or fires of home. Beyond the point of tears and blame. No lines between us. Conversation finally pointless, only the fury of antelope, jackrabbit, red tails, and peregrines. You get used to living on the edge. Is it so bad to live outside of four walls? Eventually the entire idea of home shifts altogether.

Who were we that first summer alone, father and daughter thrown upon each other toward motion against the ancient comfort of sage and rock? The few words we spoke were monumental, every glance and held hand symbolic as a smooth worn stone that felt like luck impending just around the next curve every time you felt it in your pocket. But our lives rarely have anything to do with luck.

Malheur

M Y NINE-YEAR-OLD DAUGHTER snaps open the skull of an immature deer, attempting to dislodge the sharp teeth from the jaw. She is curious. The thin hinge snaps and the calcium turns to dust recaptured by the high Oregon desert. She hands me seven teeth, a gift of remembering this quiet exchange as we turn them over and over in our hands.

I still have those teeth. They resemble piercing, miniature landscapes; steep canyon walls with uncertain, shifting summits. But in my memory they will forever be held in the small fingers of Rose.

Our entire day is given over to curiosity: discovering shy night herons in a slough swallowing orange carp; poorwills perched flat on fence posts like bumpy twigs; and white-faced ibises shy in the red willows of the Donnor Und Blitzen River. Downy owlets fade into their rocky haven. The naming of this world is important, the adding of sound to sight, and I want to pass the words on to Rose.

In an old-growth crab apple tree we find a fat porcupine. From twenty feet away we can hear him chewing his way toward the sky. When we approach he doesn't retreat or slow his eating. He is living a life I can only dream about: a life without fear.

We are moving together slowly across the landscape in search of the unexpected. We are writing our own natural history. We are only disappointed in what we can't imagine is just beyond our reach. It's not so much running as being pushed—urged—outdoors, as if it is the first day of summer, the meadowlarks have returned, and the sun hits you in the face as you lie in bed.

Circling

OUR FIRST SUMMER alone my daughter Rose discovered the Beatles. She listened to "Rubber Soul" with her usual Midwest steadiness and resolve; she asked if it was Paul, George, or John singing "Norwegian Wood." (She knows Ringo's voice.) This particular question came as we arrived in sleepy Frenchglen, Oregon, on the backside of a 2,000-mile journey that had brought us to the great eastern Oregon desert. Let me explain how we came to find ourselves in this town below the shiny sharp cliffs, tucked away at the steps of Steens Mountain, far from the madding crowds of slightly larger places like nearby Burns and Baker, and our destination of Cedarville, California, where the library is open eight hours a week, and the town has more in common with Lakeview in Oregon than California's own Sacramento.

Our nuclear family has been blown to bits. My daughter and I chose this journey for its healing potential. We are regrouping. Seeking asylum in these towns without water or playgrounds. A single parent. A single child. Father and daughter. We might be happier than this sounds.

Much of the ride, Rose stares at the ceiling of the Subaru or, more precisely, the small square cab light and at night she contemplates the amber glow of the dash. I imagine her eyes glow like a cat's. In her silence and brooding, she maintains her dignity.

She is the princess of eastern Oregon, and I am the guardian of sage and rabbit brush. We feel safe here. We have room to hurt.

Rose turned nine this summer. It is our first summer alone. Divorce is so common in our hometown that if you stick around long enough you see new relationships bordering on incest. Circles run everywhere. In one instance a man remarried his former wife's sister. It was the perfect package: complete with the same in-laws. Now and then I see all of them—ex's and kids and in-laws—wandering the streets like an exotic tribe.

On the road my quiet daughter reads incessantly, insatiably, as if all libraries are only open eight hours a week. When an antelope buck flies across the washboards of Hart Mountain, I yell to arouse her. We are both startled by the gulf between us in this small car. Perhaps we are seeing each other for the very first time.

On the day my daughter was born, in the year of the volcano, time stood still. Much to the amusement of our farm neighbors, she was born at home. I was the first to see her wet hairy back and her charcoal eyes. The day before the birth I walked in the late July dusk thinking that all the pieces of life's puzzle had fallen into place. My wife and I worked as farm hands on a sixty-cow Holstein dairy in Michigan's upper peninsula. We received milk, meat, a house, and all the diseased elms we could cut and burn free, plus $600 a month—no taxes. I spent wonderful, meditative hours on a tractor traveling in circles. Life was simple. The past was clean. No emotional dues. Sometimes I think I never lived that life.

All spring the ashy remains of Mt. St. Helens followed us east during our move to Michigan. It's as if we couldn't shake the West. And the entire time in Michigan, with the exception of Rose's birth, I never felt at ease.

We leave Frenchglen and its pastoral hotel, single phone booth, and the dead summer antelope that line the wall of a portable taxidermist stand to drive the rutted slopes of Steens Mountain. Rose and I climb the twenty miles through juniper glens on the lower reaches and twisted aspen forests near the wide summit. Winds from the top blow tough. Early August slaps bitter gales at us as we set up the tent on the shore of Honeymoon Lake. Leaves are already changing dress. Snow could fall any day.

It's a small pothole of a lake with no fish jumping and Rose soon brings me finger-sized tree frogs that she blesses with the names and attributes of her friends. Her sand-colored hair is standing on edge. The breeze carries her Lennon and McCartney love songs. She notices my stare, and returns an open smile. The gulf between us is closing here in eastern Oregon.

As the sun sets, I watch her small silhouette against the golden water. What is she thinking out there? I am overcome with love for her, this fragile being carrying the weight of adult failures. I find myself shedding the tears she has suppressed.

When we conceive our children, none of us thinks of divorce. We hope to provide them with the perfect life. Harmony and wonder. A friend once told me her greatest moments of joy— and sadness—came from her children. I chose not to take the path of least resistance. I don't want to be one of those displaced men who visit their children every other weekend, treating them to dinner at McDonald's—fulfilling the sugar-daddy role. My daughter needs me. I need her. As we zip our bags, Rose turns toward me in the half-light, snuggles close, and squeezes my arm affectionately. "Papa," she whispers, her black eyes sparkling, "are we going home tomorrow?" When I answer she is already asleep.

My Daughter's Beads

When I lack courage,
when I fear myself most,
when I drive Montana late and tired
through rain sheets and road construction,
I touch my daughter's glass beads: blue-black
with one clear piece of glass around my neck.

I'm reminded of how she took three days
in late fall of squint and delicacy;
quiet needle and thread filling the tiniest holes,
repeating for hours hunched over a pie tin.
She would not be defeated.

Now on this May evening I am alone,
driving the Blackfoot River northeast
toward Great Falls, against the drizzle,
against tight curves, against all common sense.
I may drive this highway all night.

And I am turning the beads, separating
each one with clarity. A victory, a sorrow,
a regret, a shaded truth. And I am cheered
by her gift of one white bead: compassionate,
generous against the odds.

Driving Home Alone

NORTH OUT OF Tensed, Idaho, the wheat has just a hint of the browner shades yet to come. Harvest is a month away, but the fields seem alive with activity. Today, in early July, there must be every imaginable hue of gray in the sky. Pick your weather. Lightning flashes off in the distance above the dry bluffs of Lewiston seventy miles away. The rush of wind from eastern Washington pushes my car toward the center line. The sun finds a sucker hole and spotlights a pea field. Forest meets field then retreats into shadow. Possibilities are endless.

I've been driving this eighty-three mile Moscow-Coeur d'Alene stretch of Highway 95 at least two days a week for six months and still my pulse quickens when I look for the same two red-tail hawks that sit on electrical poles above the blacktop outside the small mill town of Plummer. Since January I've watched their plumage change; seen huge ravens relentlessly hassle them in midair; and worried about them when they were absent from their poles.

Worrying about hawks: that's what the familiarity of this road does to you. It leads you to believe in the power of movement. And flight.

Tonight in Tensed ("A Quiet Place to Settle") the only cafe in town serves meatloaf sandwiches. There's not an espresso bar within forty miles. The cafe's parking lot is full with the logging and grain trucks of the families from the valley. Incomes are tight.

You work against the current and you never catch up. A night out is earned. Sons and daughters leave for Moscow, Seattle, and Spokane. You are born into the few jobs available.

It takes me exactly six minutes to drive from Worley to Plummer. A sign entering Plummer says, "The Hub of Things to Come." No doubters here. The landing at the mill holds an entire forest of raw logs on one end and blonde dimensioned boards on the other. Silhouetted shadows of the brave souls that pull greenchain rise out of the smoke and ash. Past the mill I sometimes turn onto the Old 95 cutoff. The gravel road winds under an ancient railroad trestle that displays brightly colored graffiti of past high school graduating classes. The glory years. You rarely see a freight train anymore. But there are coyotes.

I once pulled off at the top of Marsh Hill between Potlatch and Tensed, just beyond the sign that announces the beginning of the Coeur d'Alene Indian Reservation. I had just seen a coyote standing on the shoulder, frozen, as if in a daydream. When I looked back it was gone. Another time, at the same place, two snarling Dobermans ran at me out of the woods where I had stopped to stretch my legs. I barely escaped their bite. The passage over Marsh Hill is so narrow that two chip trucks approaching from different directions almost touch mirrors. Ice on the road in June is not uncommon.

I haven't mentioned the deer and the pheasants, the rainbows and sundogs, or my favorite barn. I could tell you precisely where one radio station ends and another crackles in. And how to smoothly pass a logging truck in the rain going sixty miles an hour past the turnoff to Sanders: a store, a small clutch of houses, and trailers. It's not just the contour of the highway you learn out here. It's the shape of people's lives as you move through your own. The inflection of the place. The promise that an open road brings.

After School

ose: I leave the small lamp of yellow light on for you when you return from school. I want light in the apartment with the cats and the dustballs that twirl so easily in a footstep; I want the warmth to fill you when I cannot be there. These quick years pass without pause. The collection of your school pictures grows atop the oak buffet where the light falls in a circle, and I can see all your faces, how they pass through the changes, how some years fare better than others, and I imagine how your eyes will alter with love and death. I offer you this light as the love I always carry inside for you, and I think back often to the afternoon when you, with your squinty, summer smile—dressed in a blue paisley dress, white pinafore, and tights—put your arm around me, your small, busy fingers at rest on my shoulder while someone took a picture for me to find here in my office today as I look up from my work and remember what is important. What is right about my life begins with you.

Papa

Moving Through the Landscape of Healing

A COLD, NORTHERN IDAHO September arrives with crisp, dry air from the Arctic when I take my twelve-year-old daughter to see the Canada geese camped at Spring Valley Reservoir. It is our last day together this week. Tonight she will go back to her mother and stepfather, who live in the nearby town of Deary. In the back of my car are Rose's clothes and shoes, a stuffed lamb, and a small velvet pillow filled with a pocket of fragrant mugwort given to her, as a baby, with a guarantee of sweet dreams.

I have never felt comfortable with these comings and goings. Joint custody compresses our time together into half a life. On the drive we are quieter than usual. It is safer to simply look out the windows and let protection come to us through the rapid images of fields and forests. How many times can you have your heart broken? Healing will continue today, I reassure myself as we bounce over the washboard county roads, and that healing will take place within the landscape. Maybe even redemption will occur. I do not know what Rose expects.

By the time we arrive at the lake, the restless geese have moved on. Instead, a flock of black coots occupies our investigative powers. We get out the red, well-traveled western-region edition of *Audubon Society Field Guide to North American Birds* and quickly turn to the section "Duck-like Birds." Absentmindedly, Rose keeps chanting, "black body, white beak" while she turns the slick pages past colorful pictures of buffleheads, shovelers, and lesser and greater scaups. This is the happiest work I can imagine. I look out the window, past her gold hair dissolving in the autumn colors that float beneath the ducks, and I shiver when I think of the snow to come. I am not ready for six months of Idaho frost and cold. I am not prepared for the darkness that presses down at four o'clock in the afternoon. But all my life I have not been prepared for anything that has happened.

I think back to last Memorial Day and a bird-watching tour we took at the Malheur Field Station, in the desert country of eastern Oregon. On the trip, we identified more than seventy birds, Rose jotting down their names in pencil on a page of yellow legal paper as we passed the binoculars back and forth. With more seasoned birders, we spent twelve hours a day driving around and learning how to see the obvious. It was then, at the odd, halfway age of thirty-five, that I learned the sweet, teasing song of a marsh wren and the subtle difference between a swift and a swallow. Rose said a graceful trumpeter swan landing on the Donner Und Blitzen River was her favorite sighting. We saw so much that weekend, from drumming sage grouse in the early morning, to nests with great horned owlets in downy perplexity; from a surprise whip-poor-will, concealed like a small stump, to thirty white-faced ibises in the late afternoon, waves of heat rising beneath their wings. Hundreds of white pelicans—their bills sporting the distinctive triangular bump on their upper mandible that appears only during breeding season—caught the early light from the east one morning. I have never been to Africa's Serengeti National Park, but this is how I would have imagined it—filled from horizon to horizon with wildlife.

American avocets and coots, willets, flashy western tanagers, long-billed curlews, black-necked stilts, and cinnamon teals covered the wetlands of the 185,000-acre national wildlife refuge during our stay. There was so much color, movement, and raw spring life in that vast American desert that I felt we were nineteenth-century overland pioneers or Native Americans, and the land was still empty and yearning.

How do we know where to lead our children? All I knew then—as I do now on this bright fall Sunday in our familiar Idaho stomping grounds of tamarack, white pine, and bleached basalt—is that to feel our lives again it's necessary to take Rose and me from our relative town comfort to an unpredictable landscape of open sage and paintbrush. That Memorial Day, we had birds for sky and the wetlands for imagination. I want Rose to see it all before the deserts become housing tracts and the lakes turn to sterile mud, but I don't tell her this reason. Such discoveries are personal.

When I was seventeen, immortal, with a life stretched out in long, lazy patches of slow afternoons of large clouds shadowing red southwestern mesas, I gave myself to the desert. I learned the powerful magnitude of simply being quiet, and how to slow my breath to match the rhythm of rocks. I crushed juniper berries between my palms and rubbed sage into my hair. A single day lasted beyond the rigid boundaries of time. Arizona, New Mexico, Utah, and Colorado all merged into one magical back yard, beckoning, promising, and delivering the answers to all my biggest questions. Political borders of county and state meant nothing. The great Shiprock near Four Corners became a comforting beacon in the desert's endless sea. The Los Animas River really was the river of lost souls. The La Plata Mountains meant home and the warmth of friendships and autumn potlucks. And the Apache Reservation was where I heard a mountain lion scream the neighborhood dogs into silence—an experience I have never wanted to recover from. Lost in the privilege of youth, I didn't know how fleeting those moments would become.

But like all true love that endures, it took time. I spent my very first night camping alone in an abandoned cowboy camp, tucked under a red-rock overhang in Canyonlands National Park. I was eighteen and frightened, filled with more than my share of self-doubt and anxiety, the noise of hometown Chicago still echoing through my attempted calm. On that long February night, piñon pines held the dry rattle of wind and a great horned owl kept me from resting comfortably in my sleeping bag. I was scared, scared of myself, my youth, my past, frightened of being placed among these great cliffs that resembled strange gargoyles and griffins that would outlive *me*. When I awoke the next morning from an hour's restless sleep, something had changed forever. Something at the core of who I've become today here in Idaho. As a parent. As a man. I was initiated into a world I knew nothing about. And it continues every time I step out my door and feel the first rush of breeze.

We move on to the cattails along the shore, where Rose shows me how to find shampoo hidden within the long, green stalks. I am amazed she knows this trick of stripping the cattail to reveal a sticky, clear goop. Sold for an expensive price, she says, then adds a warning: "The rest of the cattail is poisonous." We have reversed roles: this day I am the student and she is the teacher. "If you're lost in the wilderness, at least you can have clean hair." Although Rose has taught me much in the last twelve years, the lesson has never been so formal and direct. She exudes wisdom in a new way. Ten minutes ago, on the drive up here, she was quiet and sulky. But not anymore. Not outside.

We still have wild, renegade apples to pick this afternoon. With timeless regularity, the abandoned, gnarled fruit trees of northern Idaho blossom, fill, and empty without the interruption of human care. Ghost fruit. Neglected gene pools of edible apples, pears, and plums—varieties lost long ago in the hybrid shuffle of agribusiness—lie at the feet of these survivors, collecting angry, starving yellow jackets in the fall and the occasional opportunistic black bear. "Grandfather Trees," Rose once would call them, like the eighty-year-old mountain maple she would climb and swing from in the back yard at the small house of her first years. Runaway fruit is always the sweetest and snappiest, with antique tastes that even the cleverest food scientist cannot duplicate. Yet. I'm sure somewhere, someone is working on it. It is estimated that only 10 percent of the original varieties of American apples are left. Rose and I seek them out like detectives on a top-secret mission.

We have our favorite trees of other varieties, too, including the pear tree in the alley just across the street from the Moscow Public Library, and the two creaking chestnut trees in our front yard that dump their shiny load onto the street in October. As with our blackberry gleanings in the summer, it seems the choicest fruit is always the most inaccessible. In the case of the ancient tree we find, the biggest apples are guarded by two-inch thorns and hang in the upper reaches. Once again the bears have beaten us to the more accessible apples. The surrounding brown grass is matted and the lower tree limbs stripped to their green skin. Delicacy has never been a bear's virtue when it comes to eating.

I stand on my tiptoes to hit the bigger apples with a stick, and Rose runs around the tree to catch them. Because her gums are tender from her braces, I bite off chunks to give her. It reminds me of feeding her when she was a baby. There are no words for this moment, only the warmth we give each other: the unspoken support between father and daughter. The unconditional nurturing. I'm not foolish enough to disregard what this means, and I wonder what Rose will remember of these years when it has been just the two of us, what will stick to her memory. And what she'll give back to me later. Decades from now, when she eats an apple, will remembrances of this day surface as she takes her first bite?

It was almost a year ago that we made the journey back to my mother's house in Illinois. From the vantage point of 30,000 feet above ground, I showed Rose the Bitterroot Mountains, Yellowstone, Great Falls, Montana, and the Missouri River, curving and coiling upon itself. When we crossed the Mississippi somewhere over Wisconsin, I thought back to all the times I crossed that great river as a kid, riding the Union Pacific's Empire Builder out of Chicago's Union Station to my grandparents' home in Cedar Rapids, Iowa, and how that crossing seemed important to me, stepping over a boundary and out of my child's life, and how I desperately longed to ride the train past Iowa, and my waiting grandparents, west, to those towns with romantic names like Cheyenne, Denver, Whitefish, and Coeur d'Alene. At Rose's age, all I had were those names and a well-developed imagination that easily took over on those many times when reality fell short. I had never seen snow-capped mountain peaks, or rivers that weren't muddy. With its gentle motion on tracks and ties, that crossing of a great bridge was always more than enough to lift my spirit, and to carry me away.

As Rose and I waited for our flight that morning, a voice on the airport intercom urged passengers to board a plane for Detroit. The final plea said, "We are closing the door on Detroit," as if the hinges turned perfectly, the lock clicked, and everyone who did not make the boarding faced a formidable door behind which were the automobile factories of Detroit. Rose understood the silliness of such a statement. She looked at me with a slight raising of her eyebrows. That's all it takes for understanding to pass between us. I can say the word *Yellowstone* and she will nod—a tribute to an early summer camping trip when we were chased by a bull moose and failed at cooking popcorn over an open fire. Or I can say *thimbleberry* and our hands will twitch with the memory of crimson-stained fingers, and our lips tingle as we remember the tart taste of early-autumn fruit.

We sit in the quick closing of twilight, crunching apples, and I think of all the husks of abandoned homesteads in this area. Because the rolling Palouse fields resemble ocean waves, the disappearing farms take on the appearance of half-sunk ships. The same principles of atrophy apply. First the raucous winter storms strip the paint off the walls of the houses and out buildings. Structures take on the ballast of wind. Foundations shift and crack and begin to feel the weight of time pulling them into the welcoming soil. Pack rats come back on board for the final journey, building nests of oat straw and cottonwood leaves. The thin line between inside and outside dissolves with each passing season until one day it is extinguished. Not in time that is black and white, but simply exhausted into another world. The farm returns to the earth, where it belongs. Where we all belong. But the daffodils and tulips still surface each spring; the small orchard so bravely planted still endures with pink blossoms and the simple magic of fruit; and the asparagus along the ditches remains tender, sweet, and stoic.

There's more. Now and then in these Palouse fields, you'll run across a pie-sized horseshoe from the era of horse farming, when neighbors gathered together to harvest the wheat with big teams of Belgians and Shires, when hard-earned sleep came from *physical* exhaustion and the community granges were the reward, with music and dance and the enticement of courtship. I like to think those farmers felt this was enough. But I know now that here, in the shadows of abandoned homesteads and burgeoning cities, it's not. We always want more. We can't help ourselves. A lost horseshoe is the tip of remembering, the bridge between the fantasies of history and the realities of the present. Dig any deeper in the dark, wet western soil and you might not come back. And you would not be the first to disappear.

These are the moments I am moving in. As I get older, I lean more and more toward these small pockets of the obvious and the mysterious that rise from the landscape, surround my memories, and enhance a sense of possibilities. This is also where I am leading my daughter during the short years of our time together. Here, in the dense forests of northern Idaho, is where we'll make our stand. I want to unravel a thread in Rose: the thread of understanding, strength, sympathy, action, and change. The thread that weaves the fabric of humanity.

When I am an old man, with my memories replacing my future, I will remember this day and draw out its sweetness like water from a sponge: fall colors reflecting off the lake; first bite of apple; and my daughter—her spirit strong, steady, still curious—and our enduring friendship.

We toss our apple cores aside with the hopes that raccoons and badgers will benefit, then drive on and watch the first stars emerge in the darkest part of the sky—toward Montana and the eastern horizon. In a few short miles, Rose will join her mother and stepfather and be wrapped in the warm quilt of her extended family. And I will return to town, driving the slower back roads, listening for the faint cries of geese, gently guiding us with the grace of flight, as we make our journey home in the night.

Breathing

I left your door open tonight.
I wanted to hear the breathing, like the first days,
the baby days, when your breath was everything
and I listened in the deep
night hours at the foot
of your small nest of quilts
until all danger passed over
your new body. Then I could sleep.
Tonight I move restless through the hours.
Words you sing between tosses and turns
send electricity through me, a shudder.

Back then I measured your heartbeat
with my own, watched your chest rise
and fall as it took hold, took root
in the pull of the moon and tides.
I brought colors to your crib,
news of the outside world, the first taste
of apricots, the Northcoast gales.
I imagined you flew at night
with all the other babies
wrapped in white linen kimonos
above the wet rooftops of our dreary mill town.
And I would wait, ready to talk
us through this passage of dream.

Waxwings and Flickers

LATE FEBRUARY AND the Bohemian waxwings arrive in large flocks with large appetites. The flock moves as one body, working alternately between the backyard bushes and the shallow half-ice/half-slush puddles. Somewhere close by there must be a mountain ash dripping with red berries. The waxwings' broad, yellow tail bands are a hint of spring color to come. I rely on them every year to announce an end to winter's season of darkness, and like all magical events, this one is short and precious.

As they drop from the grey Idaho sky I notice dozens of red-shafted flickers accompanying the waxwings. However, they keep a safe distance at the tops of the poplar trees across the alley. What does this odd pairing mean? I have only seen flickers alone or in twos. This seems as unusual as seeing a flock of blue herons.

I open the rotting kitchen window to let all the birds' songs into our quiet apartment space. Two hundred Bohemian waxwings lift together in a perfect arc then circle and come back to their work below me. Winter is giving up, they announce. This wet Northwest snow is temporary; made up of more water than ice. Hold on to the promise of warm light and southwesterly breezes. Hold on to your dreams.

The waxwings bring it all back—the holiness and wonder of this life. Don't forsake what falls from the sky. Remember to look up. The waxwings are calling to me, urging me back to the center, back to the fold. Am I the only one who notices the birds this early morning?

Rose then walks into the kitchen on her way to get ready for school. "Papa, I'm out of cool shirts," she says dejectedly.

"Sorry," I say, looking back out at the sky. "Do you want to borrow one of mine?"

"And Papa?"

"Yes."

"Did you notice all the birds?" she asks.

I turn around and she is all smiles as she disappears into the bathroom.

The Day the Lilacs Bloom

TOWARD THE MIDDLE of May all the lilacs in this small northern Idaho town of wheat bloom at exactly the same time, creating a natural history anniversary, similar in importance to the first dusting of snow on Moscow Mountain in late fall, the gathering of bald eagles at Wolf Lodge Bay on Lake Coeur d'Alene at New Year's, and the coming of the ravenous Bohemian waxwings in late winter. It's as if a century ago all the families in town set down roots of small bushes into the dark Palouse soil on the same day with the thought that lovers, families, and poets would draw closer together on windless nights in May toward the end of the twentieth century and remember inspiration through the scent of spring.

I've endured all the usual Idaho false springs of March and April, waiting for this day: a celebration of promise, the day the entire town is sweet with the fragrance of sensuality, of opening, of lovemaking. During the day I raise up all the windows in our tiny apartment, risking the hatching yellow jackets, and in the late evening I lean out the kitchen window to face a fortress of lilacs. I inhale deeply so the white and dusty, purple-gray petals can enter the depth of my breathing down to my lungs and take root.

The night is cloudless, and the air is heavy with new spring growth. Dogs are silent. Even the suicidal moths are at rest. How can a city of 20,000 be so quiet? I write a letter to a friend and send her my most tender blessings south, like a prayer, past the lilacs to her home in Utah. I place a single petal in an envelope and imagine her in one motion slowly placing it below her nose and, without thought, whispering *lilac.*

I am restless, on the verge of everything, all at the same time, when each word and motion has consequence. My water table is high tonight and tears come up without warning. I have only felt this way in my life when I am alone or with my daughter Rose. I wish it were different. I want to feel this way every waking minute for the rest of my life. I'm ready to let down my walls and wear my heart on my sleeve.

With my head resting against the window sill I listen for the comforting sounds of home in the cool Palouse air: train whistles, night hawks, great-horned owls, footsteps down the gravelly alley. These sounds, and old wooden houses of family history, are among the last vestiges of the old West, the West before generic strip malls, franchise chicken and burger joints, and the "ticky-tacky little boxes" imported from the bowels of suburbia. Our little town has finally been discovered in the last five years. I knew the end was near when Wal-Mart and Hardees arrived.

The growth monster stalks us across the West from Durango, Colorado, to Moscow, Idaho. Beautiful places are damned. There's now a McDonalds and a Hardees in Hamilton, Montana, the final coffin nail for any small town; the two-lane road from Coeur d'Alene, Idaho, to Sandpoint, is a bumper-to-bumper recreational vehicle accident trap in the summer; the old reliable hot springs along U.S. 12 in Idaho are no longer safe from privacy and rape; and sadly, there are fewer stars visible in the night sky above Moscow. Four duplexes have been punched in on the next block, one of them replacing a garden. Gravel becomes asphalt. Traffic is unbearable in a town where most of the time there is no need to drive at all.

Maybe it's time to move farther back toward the east along with the bears, fishers, wolverines, and martens. Move back into that narrow strip of northern Rockies where all the wildness clusters and waits. Dig in and make a final stand.

Back inside I hear Rose breathing in the next room and I want to wake her up to announce the lilacs are open. She would understand the seasonal significance of such an event. Once her mother called excitedly from a phone booth late at night to alert us to the northern lights, and we were out the door within minutes driving north toward Moscow Mountain into the long, green and pink streaks of magic light. Rose didn't complain. As with most children, she welcomes the ethereal, the mystical. I understand the attraction. I want to cross over and never return.

Picture us back then from the point of view of the night above. Imagine us like a compass, pulling north, looking up, our faces bright with teal and chartreuse; the sky seamless with fields, becoming ocean then galaxy then dreamscapes. Roads become meaningless, mere non-reference points. Rose is still dressed in her night clothes. My shoes are untied and the heels crushed forward, a bad habit left over from childhood when the rush of escaping our humid Chicago apartment to friends in the alleys overtook decorum.

I believe the colors of the aurora borealis entered both of us that night. I believe we now hold these planetary shades of green like a magic serum and release them in both dreams and waking hours.

I tiptoe into Rose's bedroom and watch her sleeping as I have done every night when she is with me for more than a decade now. Her head rests on a small pillow filled with spicy mugwort, a gift from a deaf man guaranteed to guide her dreams away from nightmares. The bed is crowded with stuffed animals pressed in a variety of positions between her and the wall. Each one has a story, a life, a history. She once rescued a bald-headed doll—Alex—from a bucket of neglected toys at a thrift shop. His abandonment was real to her, as it is to all children. He needed a home, which she gave, and new clothes, which she made from scraps of cloth from the local library.

Forget that a child's stuffed animal is inanimate. Forget all you have ever known. Listen to your children breathe at night. Stand in their rooms and see their faces in moonlight. Listen to their wisdom. Then turn them loose into the fields and hills to gather lilacs.

Blankets and sheets are sprawled in all directions. Several books, mostly mysteries, are opened on the floor. Dust devils float in the corners holding spiral shapes of her hair. More piles of clothes than I will ever own. (Still, Rose announced last week that she was "low on cool shirts.") Secret notes to best friends. A locked journal. Thankfully I don't spot any ancient food.

I think of the quiet, eccentric Ruthie from Marilynne Robinson's novel *Housekeeping,* and I think of my own disheveled youth when my room looked no different than my daughter's does tonight, and how I would go for days without talking to anyone. I gave up long ago on the importance of housekeeping. Messy bedrooms convey an order of creativity, like spring runoff on the Selway River or an old-growth forest in the high Siskiyous of northern California. Trim lawns and spotless houses convey a brand of control I've never been able to sustain.

During the first scary days of marital separation I resumed the habit of reading out loud to Rose before bed. We needed a connection to words, to familiar territory. It was hard to face each other with all our fears and rage, but facing a page of words felt safe. Everything was so brittle then. Even breathing was fractured.

One night I read from *The Stolen Appaloosa,* a book of Nez Perce legends. The story "The Girl and the Dog" is a tale of an Indian princess who refuses the many suitors brought to her. She instead takes a dog as her partner and lives happily ever after. I understand the ending. A friend once said to me, after her husband had stormed out after a fight, "That's it. I'm getting a piano, a horse, and a dog, and I will be trading up!" Music and animals: trading up indeed.

Rose followed the sentences across the pages and politely told me when I skipped a word. Her head rested on my chest and I held her tight. I didn't ever want to let go.

Some nights Rose sleep walks. I have sometimes been startled from my dreams to find her standing next to my bed—eyes open—her voice a mixture of mirth and distress. She will continue to talk to me as I guide her back to her room. The next morning she remembers nothing. Other nights I hear her sing or laugh or cry. She maintains a pre-birth connection to the other world, no less real than the waking one.

I turn from her doorway, suddenly hear a low rumbling in the distance toward the Snake River bluffs by Lewiston and understand why the night is so still. It's the prelude of calm. Thunderstorms are rare on the Palouse and they are usually far in the distance. Flashes of electricity descend from the Wallowa Mountains in northeastern Oregon. Our apartment is suddenly bright with white light. Rose stirs under the covers.

Rose is a child of green sky, thunder, and summer downpours. It's the Midwest in her. During the buildup of low pressure she will lie on her bed with her face almost completely out her bedroom window searching for those first few fat drops of warm rain. The electricity goes right to her soul and she is at her happiest.

Another flash of light. The low rumble louder now, moving north toward this small room. More stirring. Rose's sleepy dream voice. I catch the intoxicating fragrance of lilacs.

I slide down along the doorway and sit looking past Rose out to the south, alternately watching her face (passing from dark to white) and the lilac bushes out her window near the alley. This must be every parent's perfect moment: watching a child asleep and safe from all the storms of the world outside. Listening to the rise and fall of breathing. In this room there is only a present tense to our lives together. I've been through enough to know this kind of peace is rare and fleeting. This is all I've ever asked of life: just to be here, to achieve this humble goal of harmony, to observe first-hand the influence of low pressure and electricity on my young daughter, to smell lilacs and the coming rain, to move beyond economics and consumption into dream work, to live as if this life is an open window in spring. To want only what we have. I close my eyes and whisper, "it is more than enough." In agreement, the rain arrives, slapping against the eaves, filling the air, changing everything.

Swimming with My Daughter

You don't notice the crawdads at first.
Prehistoric eyes and antennae.
Their movement makes no sense.
But you would know the sound
they make when crushed.
Like eating undercooked corn on the cob.
They sense our feet in the warm water.
Always the biggest rear up to pinch.
Smaller ones twist into torpedoes,
exploding the sand beneath our toes.
You don't suspect a thing.

When finally you see them,
you refuse the shore,
jumping on my shoulders in happy panic.
Fearful yet glad for this adventure.
Every rock teems with creeping crustaceans.
Bubbles announce an attack.
When a stick brushes your knee
the canyon echoes with your screams.
Like a miner's wife who went mad
with winter.

While you shiver in my arms
I tell you about last summer:
when I woke a black bear
just behind those tamaracks
where the cheatgrass is still matted.
But no crawdads that afternoon.
Only what the raccoons left
bleached on the basalt.

We float further out, toward safe water
both afraid now to touch bottom.
Each nursing our secret fears.
Listening to the rocks move.

Kamiak Butte

S PRING HAS PUSHED us out the door into the forests and fields of Latah County. Yesterday, on a drive in the eastern part of the county, we were overwhelmed by constant carpets of shooting stars, trilliums pushing up through the dampness; camas, buttercups, fairy slippers, and everywhere water rushing down the divide, west, to the merging of sand and salt. Birds have returned, too. Red-winged blackbird and meadowlark songs compete for airspace. Ring-necked pheasants search for hiding places on the edges of new wheatfields. We spot two yearling moose foraging in the debris of clearcuts behind the town of Clarkia. Snow blocks our attempts to seek the higher reaches above the Little North Fork of the Clearwater River. Like every year, we are too early; too anxious to climb out of our winter skins, too hungry for sun.

Spring is the great reminder of how life endures against the greatest of odds: thick frost, deep snow, drought, environmental devastation. Our internal landscape holds the same threats to survival as our external landscape of rivers, earth, and sky. Against tremendous odds we continue in a struggle to seek a perfect balance of the social and the personal. But these are tenuous lives we lead. Can a heart exist without the nourishment of love? Is there a word for a mind filled with silt, or a spirit in desperate need of warmth? A new vocabulary is in order. A lexicon that describes how we react to the opening of lilacs or to the absence of breeze just before a prairie thunderstorm. Or the feeling that arises when a favorite landmark of landscape is suddenly razed.

In the same way as the yearling moose, like the wild onions and bachelor buttons rising out of the grey, Rose and I have survived another winter of early darkness. We are over the equinoctial hump. In the tender shoots of yellow-green grasses we are still standing. It is the most courageous act we will ever commit, simply going on.

Two things that Rose did in the past week took me by surprise. When I came home from work she was singing to herself while washing the dishes. She didn't hear me walk in so I paused silently at the doorway to listen. The song was one from her school choir. Her back was to me; she was facing the back alley with the budding lilacs and tall poplar trees that are often filled with flickers. Water was splashing everywhere. The kitchen was alive with music. She was in the best of moods, feeling the freedom of being alone, but safe, and traveling through the reaches of a musical landscape. Who knows what she was thinking as she slid the dishes under the warm suds, or what hopes she was creating at the time. I want desperately to learn what moves my daughter, but you can only know a person so well. Some moments are so private and perfect it is best not to interfere. Privacy requires space. I quietly closed the door and walked around the block so she could have a few more minutes of song and expanse.

That same week, Rose buried her hamster, who set a record in the household by living for three years. (That is, if you don't count the hamster that simply disappeared into the secret alcoves of our apartment. The cats were strangely silent and content during our searching.) On her own Rose placed the stiff hamster in a cream cheese container, and using the claw end of a hammer, dug a small hole in the back yard where she solemnly placed her corpse. She then covered the grave with dirt and placed two bricks on top. I watched from the kitchen window. It was a simple ceremony and it had to do with creating her own ritual. She stood over the tiny mound for a moment and said some words I couldn't hear.

Kamiak Butte in nearby eastern Washington is 298 acres of perfection. Named for Chief Kamiaken, a Yakima Indian, Kamiak is a tall, granite landmark on the Palouse; a forested break from the cultivated farm fields below it. One of the perennial first stops in our celebratory swing through this new season, I've always thought of the cluster of larch, pine, and fir as a bio-regional ship floating in a sea of wheat. It's the perfect vantage point in which to contemplate direction without the interference of artificial political boundaries. To the west I imagine the scablands, then the Cascades, the long chain of volcanoes that run from California's Mt. Lassen north to Mt. Baker in Washington. I imagine the calm tidepools of the Pacific and the raucous outlet of the Columbia River at Astoria, Oregon. Looking south I think of Whitebird Hill, the Seven Devils Mountains, the Wallowas where Chief Joseph was driven away from his home, the canyonlands surrounded to the east by the La Sal Mountains, which have a bluish tint to them in the fall. North I see grizzly bears and the small caribou band of the Selkirk range, the Canadian Rockies, the source of the Columbia River. The arctic. When I face east I remember the Bitterroots, the Continental Divide, Big Hole Battlefield, the Midwest where my family comes from, the Great Lakes, and northern Michigan where Rose was born. It's as if my history stretches out in front of me. When I close my eyes and lean into the winds I can go anywhere I wish.

When I climb to the top of Kamiak and look out I am reminded of Moscow writer Carol Ryrie Brink, who described the

Palouse in her book of memoirs, *A Chain of Hands:* "I . . . ride my pony between wheat fields and dusty hedges of long-lost wild roses; hear meadowlarks like chimes on lonely fenceposts, and distant church bells like flying birds. I see the tall Lombardy poplars that are now cut down, and smell the keen scent of wet, new lumber or rotting leaves. I see the blue mountains beyond the yellow wheatfields. . . ."

On Kamiak the wild onions are up, along with the orange and red paintbrush. Soon the ocean spray will hang down the paths like wisteria and blossom overnight. Then the wild strawberries, bachelor buttons, huckleberries, yarrow, and thimbleberries will appear in late summer. These flowers, shrubs, and berries are anchors in our sense of place. Year after year we reassess ourselves against their appearance.

Later in the summer, when the creeks slow their flow and warm to the long hours of sun, Rose and I go swimming in the big pools of Potlatch Creek. We have two favorite swimming holes, using one as a backup when the other is taken. Born during Midwest rain, Rose is a natural swimmer. Our routine is to pick the hottest afternoon, then drive slowly along the creek assessing the depth of the water as we go. We pack towels, ice water, and books, maybe some fruit. On the return trip we stop at the Town and Country Cafe in Kendrick for the best milk shakes in the county. Nights after we swim we sleep like logs, both snoring from our bedrooms.

When we stand still in the lukewarm water, hundreds of minnows appear and suck at our bare legs. Each year we marvel at the ingenuous homes of the caddisflies that live at the bottom of the ponds: one-inch cylinders, encrusted with the tiniest of pebbles, garnets, and mica. Occasionally a kingfisher works the creek, or a pair of mallards wobble through. Once we came upon thousands of crawdads in the creek, causing us to forego our swimming that day. Always there is the threat of rattlesnakes but we have only ever seen one.

As with Kamiak Butte, it's the sameness that draws me back to Potlatch Creek, a reliance upon natural history to guide me through this life. Against these backdrops, I can remind Rose of years past, or direct her toward the future. There's nothing un-usual about my decision to take her out into the landscape. It might even be hereditary. My mother once said, "Whenever I feel down I think about trees. They're so courageous, losing all their leaves in the fall and trusting that in the spring their leaves will return."

And it was Walt Whitman who wrote, in *Song of Myself*, "Space and Time! now I see it is true, what I guess'd at, What I guess'd when I loaf'd on the grass, What I guess'd while I lay alone in my bed, and again as I walk'd the beach under the paling stars of the morning."

Remembering Lulu Pearl

LILACS STILL CLING to their blooms when we head to the cemeteries. It's a curious passion of Rose's, one that I share and encourage, although for different reasons. I read the inscriptions, take pictures, and rearrange the plastic flowers. Rose rubs the headstones of infants as if reassuring them they will be remembered through her small hands.

Latah County has its share of rural resting places and we're equipped with the best backroad map of the county, each cemetery flagged by a small symbol of a headstone. Because we believe in goals, our plan is to eventually visit every graveyard in the county.

We visit these graveyards for another reason. In addition to the obvious solitude and the last remnants of native plants such as bunchgrass, cemeteries are the remaining bastions of non-development in the community. We are assured that these quiet refuges will not be excavated, subdivided, and covered with generic, six-figured, often poorly designed and built homes most of us will never afford. Cemeteries are also natural settings for mourning and increasingly I've been mourning the vanishing landscape of the Palouse.

On this spring afternoon, Rose spots a cluster of tumbled, white stones on a knob of a hill and we make a beeline up the washboard road bordered by bluebells, mule ears, and the first tall white stalks of yarrow. A black and white dog greets us and offers a stick. I pull to a stop and Rose jumps out and quickly disappears into the mass of pine trees and hedges. I won't see her for an hour. I don't worry about her.

I read about Lulu Pearl, foster daughter of S.D. and C.I. Oylear, born August 2, 1898, only to die January 15, 1904. "Here rests the sweetest bud of hope that e'er to human wish was given." For Caroline, wife of Marion Rogers: "As a wife devoted, As a mother affectionate, As a friend, ever kind and true." Nancy Jane: "Aged 35 years, 3 months, and 19 days." A precision that brought a kind of finality of solace. The dead comfort the living and the living continue with the dead on parallel paths.

There are younger deaths, like Baby Jack, who died after two days of life: "Our darling one hath gone before to greet us on the blissful shore." On Baby Jack's bleached stone is a pair of lambs guarding a clutch of purple irises. I look across the yard and read the names Alva, Matilda, Minnie, Oscar, Mattie, Addison, Salla, Hattie, Flora Levina, and Abrham.

I crouch forward, part a sprig of bluebells to reveal a lichen-covered headstone and whisper, "Here's a baby." Suddenly Rose is next to me and holds a spray of flowers. "Here's kitten ears."

I may be wrong, but Rose seems to understand how life and death share the same world. She is not afraid. There are so many spirits here, so much death, but I don't feel any sadness, not with the dog tagging along, my daughter moving easily among the leaning stones and plastic flowers, rubbing the words with her palms as if offering her touch. I imagine her thinking, "You are not forgotten. Talk to me, tell me your stories. I'll tell you mine."

The stories are universal. They are plain truths we all share. Couples buried side by side, dying within a few months of each other. A heart disease of another type when the heart breaks and there is not enough time for healing to occur.

"To live in the hearts we leave behind is not to die."

Divorce leads to heartbreak, too, and a death, but somehow the grave remains uncovered. When I decided to give up on my marriage I wrote the following words to Rose, hoping to mend her small heart, but knowing I couldn't: "You are not to blame. This has nothing to do with a messy room or talking back or not finishing your vegetables. I can see you withdrawing already into books and fast images on color screens. It's safer with your stories and your cats. All I can offer is this: I was once in your place and I know about this type of pain. Hold on. Although it may not seem like it right now, you will survive and you will go on. Besides, it's all you can do. I will always be here for you and that was more than was offered me."

In the cluttered miners' cemetery above the ghost town of Elkhorn, Montana, sits a bleached headstone with these words etched across the front: "No pains, no griefs, no anxious fears can reach our loved ones sleeping here."

Where My Daughter Walks at Night

On a night when the moon will burst
my daughter talks of cemeteries. She believes
souls of the dead can suck a child under
the soil when the wind is a voice calling.
So she tiptoes between headstones
and holds her breath. And listens.
I never go with her, but I hear
the door close in the early morning
and wet footsteps past my room.
She empties her pockets into a music box
that plays popular waltzes, lies down
across the bed with the cats, caked river mud falling
from her shins, red oak leaves braided in her hair.
When I enter the room to call her to breakfast
she is reading. And speaking to no one.

Steens Mountain

ALL DAY WE MOVE past the hot back roads of Oregon's antelope desert. We are running toward comfort in towns of permanent drought. Towns without children. Rose counts license plates from her back seat bed. She is searching for identity in the names of states: Connecticut. Georgia. U.S. Government. We almost never talk except to share this information.

It's important to us. We tell no one.

Each night we make camp, drinking soup from tin plates, warm milk from plastic cartons, and sucking sugar cubes for sweet dreams.

"Papa, we are hoboes," she says, her black eyes dancing. And she reaches for my arm, asleep now, as I listen for bears.

On the west slope of Steens Mountain, we hike the stunted aspen forest the locals call Whorehouse Meadows. I read the graffiti of wine goblets and genitalia, exaggerated through the swell of decades. Grown tall beyond our reach now. The sheepherders came from Frenchglen. The women were brought from Burns.

I imagine loneliness in these scarred trees. Rose sees white bark, first blush of summer's passing. She takes my hand—tight with sweat—and leads me away from the ghosts. "Let's go, Papa."

At nine she knows nothing of this brand of sorrow or how loneliness can eat away at you like a form of cancer. But she knows of loss and how fragile home is.

From that same forest of white bark my daughter captures tree frogs the size of thumbs, and whispers the melody wind plays through bent limbs.

Selway River

"NOTHING IN THIS WORLD is plain." I read that line today, here, surrounded by the wet fertility of the Idaho Bitterroots; the incense smell of ancient cedars in a 12,000-year-old inland climax rain forest. The smell of home, really: the five-fingered ferns held together by delicate, black stems, wild ginger, fiddlenecks and western sword ferns, elegant dogwoods, the gentle, endless roar of a creek—water over rocks, smoothing out the rough edges. So simple to grasp: this stream is melted snow falling with gravity, mixing with a dozen rivers until it tastes salt at the Pacific Ocean. This I understand. This makes sense. Or so I think. How much do I truly understand about the natural world?

I watch the mid-morning sun search out last night's torrent of mountain rain. Soon the heat will reach me, dry the bench where I sit quietly, and the damp tent where my daughter Rose sleeps on, her body tired from the rapid growth of pre-teen years. I give her this long rest along the creek because soon she will rise at seven each morning for school. And because this morning I want bird song to permeate her dreams and infiltrate her memories.

Last night in the plunging barometrical heave of an impending thunderstorm we found a dead hummingbird. Rose passed it to me—small hand to large hand, this warm pocket of bird, lighter than a fountain pen and half the size. Tiny feet folded underneath bright, greenish-auburn feathers with a neon radiance.

No blood, no visible cause of death. When I hold it this morning the body is still soft and elastic without death's usual stiffness and smell of decay. Maybe the internal biological life had left through the empty eye sockets, leaving this colorful husk intact. Bird colors never fade. Another miracle. Nothing in this world is plain.

I wrap the hummingbird in a damp paper towel and place it in the Coleman. For the rest of the trip Rose will roll her eyes with exasperation each time she opens the cooler lid to get slices of cheese.

Inside our freezer at home: rough-legged hawk wings, ring-necked pheasant feathers, an orange shafted flicker tail, a stiff talon wrapped in soft deerskin. I bring them inside our home from ditches, peel them off center lines; from grain truck grills and barbed wire. I cannot get enough of feathers. They demand dignity.

"Papa, our freezer is like a zoo," Rose said once, fetching ice cubes and juice.

"Cold kills the microorganisms," I said in defense. "No maggots this way." But she knows I am preserving sky, hanging onto wildness. A form of greed.

Now the weak morning canyon light has found my body. I shiver away last night's chill. Soon Rose will awaken. I can still predict her movements beforehand, though not as acutely as when she napped in her first baby years. Instinct—how it persists despite the pressures against it. When Rose would cry in those first few months of life, her mother's breasts would leak and soak her blouse as her milk involuntarily let down.

I place the hummingbird in the sunlight hoping its eyes will fill the empty sockets, its tiny wings will flutter and spread, the chest will fill with air, and talons will find a safe perch. I believe it is possible on this morning in the forest, in the primeval light that is always changing.

White Pelicans

If yearning could be measured in wingspan
it would be this cluster of birds, draped
in cumulus white under a grey cover
of drizzle sky that could only be Montana

in June. And an impossible current
that masks the rich world beneath
this floating island of feathers.
What is it about these twenty birds

that brings the word *vulnerability*
to the lips? The way dim sunlight
filters orange through their thin bills
I trust entirely in crossing over.

Maybe I haven't been awake
until this instant. Or spent enough
time alone in the cold, spring mud
in genuflection of flight.

Maybe today I'll learn
what it means to be alive,
finally surrounded, in the middle
of everything all at once.

Madison River

ON OUR LAST NIGHT on this July swing through Idaho and Montana I wonder what Rose and I have accomplished. How do I measure this movement through landscape? Each night we camped along a majestic Western river: the Selway, the Blackfoot, the Madison. We fell asleep to their soothing movement; felt the rivers' current pull beneath our sleeping bags; heard the last evening birds, the nocturnal silence; then the first morning birds commence their songs as they worked the waters' reedy edges.

There is so much activity on these waters. When I went for pans of coffee water from the Blackfoot I was met by an osprey gently carrying a trout in its talons, both of them facing in the same direction, as if the bird was showing the fish the landscape from the sky. *Here is the world I live in.*

Sometimes I hear voices or music but no one is there.

Nothing in this world is predictable. We see a flock of turkey vultures on fence posts near Ovando, Montana, waiting to clean up on death. Coming over Lolo Pass, Rose spots a moose moments after I spot a wild turkey. And then, rounding a curve along the Madison River, a bright, cumulus white cloud of feathers and arched, flesh-colored bills and necks. Western white pelicans moving through twilight as a group, feeding, preening, large as trumpeter swans, huddled against the constant drizzle.

I jerk the emergency brake, jump out of the car, crouch in the mud on the road with binoculars. Rose stays seated but looks over my shoulder. She is hungry and tired. I have promised her cheese tortellini in tomato sauce with fresh French bread "soakers" bought in Helena that afternoon. I am trying her patience. We both know the limits of what friendship can endure and I am at the boundary, pushing. But she will allow me my pelicans, my indulgence for birds. She knows why I am on my knees in the cool downpour. A supplication for pelicans. A prayer for these white angels that bring the sky to us. Winged reminders to look above our own lives into cloud space.

Usually Rose rolls her eyes when I go on one of my tirades against road kills of hawks and owls; when I rail against the encroachment of malls and the absence of community. But here on the Madison River she is kind to me in her waiting. In all probability the two of us will never see fifteen pelicans on this river again. Odds are against it. In any case, why not live this moment as if it is our last time with birds?

In the evening as we set up camp on the Madison, Rose comes back to life. I assign tasks to both of us. She's in charge of unraveling sleeping bags, inflating air mattresses, arranging pillows and flashlights. I'll make dinner. Together we raise the tent. Our camp is almost in the river, surrounded by red willow bushes that frame the gauzy Madison like a Russell Chatham painting. We could take three steps and be swept away in the fast currents and not be found for days.

In the cold night air are the soothing cries of birds on the fly: the squawk of the blue heron, legs outstretched like a second parallel beak; the high pitched call of a lone killdeer; and the almost soundless, anonymous brush of wings in the dark. This night every living thing—river included—seems to be on the move: the birds, the black clouds to the south coming out of Yellowstone, the increasing velocities of the wind. Everything, that is, but us.

We listen to the hum of the little stove, taking turns stirring the curly pasta, finally giving in to our hunger and tasting too early. It's a perfect evening. Rose's cheeks are bright crimson—baby red. She is wearing one of my oversized pullover sweaters, her hands disappearing into the big sleeves. She is smiling with independent mischief. Independence has been her strongest characteristic and she handles it with a responsible edge. Rose is as stubborn as I am and not afraid of solitude. Will she someday realize the immense freedom in being alone, and the difference between solitude and loneliness?

"She will be OK," I say to myself. "She will have a good life."

The river light quickly fades as we adjust the tension of the rain fly with smooth river rocks. As the pasta simmers we huddle together on the ground using the cooler to support our backs and double as a poor windbreak. Fire from the butane stove lights our cheeks. We have driven more than 400 miles to be here together.

Out here Rose and I have the space to face each other. It's these quiet moments when I feel most like a father, when patience returns within the familial atmosphere of listening, understanding each word that is spoken between us. Clarity. This is the measure of my life. This is what I bring to the world: my ability to listen to my daughter.

On this trip I can teach Rose the important lessons: how the heavy rain clouds from the Pacific dump their moisture along the Lochsa and Selway watersheds in the Bitterroots creating a landlocked rain forest, hundreds of miles from salt water. I tell her the climate is the same as the coast and the dogwood trees are proof. On the cobble banks of the Lochsa River in Idaho, we stand looking up knowing we cannot see the tops of trees. Instead we touch the soft, mossy bark, and imagine. I show Rose wild ginger, get her to smell. There is the Nez Perce tobacco, kinnikinnick, and the state flower of Idaho, syringa, or mock orange. Snowberries and horsetail. Snails that Rose whispers encouragement to and feeds pinches of French bread.

Here is a way to measure time: five hundred-year-old cedar trees in a twelve thousand-year-old forest with a twelve-year-old daughter.

Listen to this river. I am giving my mind and body to the power of the Madison (Let it sweep us away!), the Mad, the Blackfoot, Selway, Eel, Smith, Klamath, Salmon—all the great rivers I have loved. Is there more comfort than this sound, this gravitation of wave over rock nestled between two banks? Everything I love is within three simple steps, my daughter, birds, and a river.

Roiling currents of the Madison move beneath our bodies with such power that as we fall asleep I tell Rose we are floating in the water with the pelicans; that I don't know where we will be in the morning, and that tonight I really don't know anything at all. She doesn't answer. There is only the sound of her breathing, heavy, as if she were putting down roots in the river.

Continental Divide

I try to explain to my daughter
how water slides off the tips
of green mountains near Wisdom, Montana,
with equal pull.
East, toward her Michigan birthplace,
the five big lakes the shape of herons lifting.
West, toward her mother, Oregon's sand
dunes then ocean waves. Horizon's ledge.

She's quiet, shrugs under sun shades,
watches the land peel away at sixty miles per
out the car window, faster near the sticky pavement,
higher, the sky moves slow as rocks. She studies
what I've said, gives back silence
so my words fill the car, press against
shut glass, hot dashboard, our still hands.

There is no movement of water in any direction
no glimmering mirages
to prove the lesson of divide.
Who can be sure we are near an edge
when the road beneath us whispers
the steady resolve of movement
and the sun chases us backward, falling.

Living for Swans

A MAN AND A WOMAN sweep the dust from the treeless main street of Wisdom, Montana. At first this seems a foolish task, given over to those with too much time on their hands and an unhealthy desire for tidiness. But if the dust was allowed to settle what would this tiny outpost resemble? The couple push the dust west toward Idaho; the wind picks it up and deposits it right back at their feet. But I sense progress somehow. And dignity.

Rose and I could tell them a thing or two about dust, and dirt, maybe even dignity, as we watch them through the plate glass window at Fetty's Cafe where the loud locals and timid out-of-towners gather for the morning coffee ritual. We have just spent a night camping out near the Continental Divide just east of Lost Trail Pass, at the southern end of the Bitterroot Valley, where the valley scales the blistered "thumb" of eastern Idaho. Our hips are sore from sleeping on the ground and rolling east in our sleep from the pull of the divide. We are covered with Montana forest duff and road dust, and because it is June in Montana—a winter month out here—even the dust is cold.

Rose has just completed fourth grade, and has been released for the summer on good behavior. We have abandoned town suddenly, without any advance bragging, for a trip out of Moscow is always viewed with envy in early summer. Landscapes of mountains and valleys call to us. Like an interior compass they point us east to Yellowstone. East to cold, smoldering, blackened forests from the previous year's great fires. The Coleman cooler is packed with cold pasta salad, seltzers, candy bars, dry Italian salami, the sharpest cheese with the highest fat content found anywhere in the Northern Rockies, and, as a marginal nod to good health, milk. One percent.

The night before we left I reread Montana poet Richard Hugo's poem, "Driving Montana": "The day is a woman that loves you. Open." Throw our tattered Rand McNally across a room twice and it will fall open to one of two states: Idaho or Montana. I believe the distances printed in the atlas for Idaho are fairly accurate, but those for Montana are underestimated. A geographical fool's gold. Rand McNally devotes two pages to Montana, and, no matter how many days I drive, I can never get to the second page.

I could not pack fast enough. Sleep is a distant memory lately. I am emotionally tired, with the unease of depression, guilt, and sloth, my three internal traveling companions. My Wise Men. This single-parenting and forty-hour work week is wearing me out; keeping me from being a good parent. I feel my heart banging loudly against my chest and listen for a minute; I stop counting at ninety beats.

Adding to my own historical anxiety is an additional inherent insecurity to traveling alone with a young child, similar to camping alone. Uneasy questions surfaced as we drove up the Bitterroot Valley: What if something happens to me? Can Rose get help? Could she use a phone in an emergency? Did I remember to give her a quarter and the necessary important phone numbers to keep in her pocket? As if on cue my lower back starts to ache. Now on which side is the appendix?

Bridging the gap between my worst-case imaginings and Rose's hopeful nine-year old spirit is perhaps my biggest challenge as a parent. I want to caution her about life's real dangers, but without destroying her trust in the goodness of the human heart. I want her street smart, but I don't want to scare her away from taking chances. She should be able to walk dreaming in the night air, to camp alone in a Western forest under Orion's Sword, and lean forward toward wilderness. How do I teach sanity and security in a world that continues to move away from both?

Inside Fetty's Cafe, dust tracked over the threshold forms paths that lead to the booths. A giant, lacquered blue marlin fills an entire wall. Two-month-old newspapers lie everywhere, filled with the usual overwritten and under-crafted wire stories: a new prison in Crescent City, California; the debate over flag burning; and a poll showing that 53.5 percent of Israeli men purchase their own socks.

We eat our eggs and pancakes quietly, conscious of our status as strangers. Rose ignores the marlin, the news, maybe even our surroundings, choosing to read a Babysitters' Club book instead. She is far away from the classrooms of Russell Elementary School back in Moscow; far from her friends, some of whom are on their way to Disneyland, with its hotels and fancy pools and fast-food restaurants. There is no fast food or fast anything in Wisdom, Montana. We are nowhere glamorous. Between pages, she looks up at me across the table and smiles.

"How are you doing, Rose?" I ask, wanting some long answer filled with fourth-grade wisdom; an Epiphany as to why we are here in this small-town cafe. I want my daughter to be exuberant, cheerful, and chatty—everything I'm not. As usual I want too much. I want to know what to expect.

"Are we near Yellowstone?" she asks, looking serene as if it is no surprise that she was suddenly plucked from the pages of her book to this cafe scene.

"Just a few more hours, Rose. We're almost there."

She returns to her book. I count the fins on the marlin, listening to the sound of the two brooms sliding across the asphalt.

I pick the northern entrance—the oldest entrance—into Yellowstone, careful not to spend one cent in the gaudy tourist ruination of Gardiner, Montana, with its inflated gasoline prices and Taiwanese plastic buffaloes (Whose culture is this?), instead feeling like Mary Lennox in *The Secret Garden* as we pass under the Roosevelt Arch into the park, beneath the words, "For the Benefit and Enjoyment of the People."

"I am safe now," I say under my breath. "I'm at home base. They cannot find me now. Not here." A friend has a saying that once seemed outrageous and cowardly, but is now my motto. "There is no problem big enough you can't run away from."

This June I am trying to run away from myself.

I contemplate new solitary careers, careers that preclude broken promises and joint counseling: sheep herder above ten thousand feet, precipitation-gauge monitor in the Bitterroots, ptarmigan researcher, those sorts of jobs. Monasteries are beginning to look appealing.

Another, more important, goal has brought us to Yellowstone: I want to show Rose there is an order to the natural world—an order of flowers and birds and bison, an order that can change at any moment. I'm ambitious this summer. I will continue to teach her to love the land. I want to nurture in her a sense of possibilities, a belief in hope. Here at Yellowstone—a park dedicated by Ulysses S. Grant in 1872—far away from the clatter of our self-inflicted artificial nonsense of economy, within the heart of a landscape, possibilities still abound. Somewhere out here where the spaces are not yet filled in is an honest country absent of billboards and corporate endorsements. Looking around, I see every shade of green and blue, and the glorious richness of brown and grey. And black—the color of loss and mourning.

Just last week, Rose told me that she wanted to study animals, but then quickly added, "but there probably won't be any left when I grow up." Her small heart needs mending. I need to show her there is still a place where animals are somewhat plentiful—and safe.

Soon Rose will draw on the lunar landscape of tides and moons for strength and be just as unpredictable and mysterious as the last wild wolves of Montana. She will need these vast ranges of bison and elk in which to stretch out her soul. It's not simply a "solace of open spaces." It's raw sustenance and most of the time it's a source of restlessness as well as peace.

Where will our children learn to love the landscape if it does not start with us, their parents? We have left the greatest lessons of life in the hands of those who do not love or value our children except as future consumers.

Our first night in Yellowstone is spent crowded in a campsite between tents and trailers. I foolishly try to boil water with the weak flame of Sterno, and dinner takes longer than either of us expects. Still there is a peacefulness at this campground I've been seeking for months. Our goals this evening are modest: put up a tent, unroll pads and sleeping bags, make dinner, take a walk along the nearby stream, and turn in early. Why did it take so many years to come here?

At dusk, while the pasta inhales and spits, our camp neighbors—three men in their twenties—come back from a short hike with news that a cow moose and her calf are browsing down by the stream. They have returned for their cameras. Rose wants to investigate, but I don't want her to go alone and I can't leave our supper cooking on an open fire, no matter how weak the flame. I also know she may never have this opportunity again.

The men offer to take Rose—it's a short ways, they assure me. I look into their eyes and see endless stretches of kindness. Now and then you have to trust, I tell myself. If the human spirit can't shine here in these ancient woods, then we are all doomed to lives of paranoia and fear. I relent.

As they disappear into the woods I wonder if I have done the right thing. But she returns fifteen minutes later full of exuberant descriptions of the moose and her baby. She is full of fresh confidence. This will forever be *her* experience, one that only she can recount: the time when, on her own, without parental guidance, she saw her first moose.

"Papa, you have to see this," she almost shouts.

The next night, after dinner and a failed attempt at making popcorn on an open fire, Rose and I take our evening hike up Slough Creek. She's dressed in a nine-year-old's version of elegant evening apparel: red pajamas and black sneakers with two sets of colored shoe laces left fashionably untied.

We pass three elk carcasses on our way back to where it feels wild, back to where the trail becomes a vague whisper and the woods are tumbled "like a forest should look," I tell Rose. Fresh grizzly droppings confirm we have crossed a boundary of sorts between the tents back at the campground and the great forests of Yellowstone. We instinctively become quiet.

We don't turn back.

As we continue, slower and even quieter now, I spot a bull moose browsing in the middle of the raging waters of Slough Creek. Rose, who has left her glasses back at the camp, cannot quite see him. The moose disappears behind a brushy island near our side of the bank. We hurry in that direction, hoping to get a good view of him still lounging in the water, but as we round a bend in the trail, there he stands—ears back like a cat in fight stance. In a matter of seconds he will charge.

I yell at Rose to get off the trail, thinking if we give the moose a wide berth he won't feel threatened. Rose is frightened. "I don't want to be here, Papa," she cries out, rushing ahead of me. I don't agree. I think we're fortunate to be stumbling through this thick underbrush together, hearts bursting, adrenalin surging, scrambling for our very lives.

I find a large, fallen ponderosa pine. "He won't come in here," I tell Rose, although I'm not entirely sure this is true. "He only wants the trail." The moose pauses, then, poor eyesight and all, passes by, a mere silhouette in front of us. Frisky and full of himself, he charges back across the creek up the opposite bank, moving away from us, into the dusk, leaving us to collect and reassemble ourselves.

I squeeze Rose's hand. "Are you all right?" I ask.

She nods and rises slowly beside me still crouched on my knees. The only sound is the creek, growing louder as the night grows darker. She stares over my shoulder into the forest, almost looking through me. Wherever she is now, she is alone, gathering strength. She has been touched by wildness and survived.

After a few more minutes of silence, it is Rose who starts back to the campground first. There is no hurry in her step. She walks with confidence, leading the way, as if she knows this forest. She is moving in time with the rhythm of the creek, belonging to her surroundings. Belonging to no one.

Later that night in our small tent, Rose tosses and turns, alternately speaking and laughing, as if she is channelling. At one point she sits straight up in her sleeping bag, eyes open, still pursued by the moose. I reach over to touch her, and talk to her soothingly.

"You are safe, Rose. The moose is far away now. Papa's right here. Now go back to sleep."

She is rigid—hard as marble. Then she gives in. Her white knuckles relax, take on their natural color, finally holding on to nothing.

I step quietly out into the night air through a pyramid of stars in the tent's opening and instinctively look up at the Milky Way. I need to breathe deep and fill my lungs with stars. Whenever I walk into the forest I feel like I have just woken up. Life indoors, enclosed within the clutter of a modern world, is the dream.

Tonight, as on most nights, I begin a one-sided dialogue with my daughter.

Everything seems fragile tonight, Rose. Here's the situation: We have only thin layers of nylon and goose down to insulate us from the frigid Montana night. Four rubber tires. Four old pistons. Three twenty-dollar bills. No credit cards. More grizzly bears than pay phones. We almost got trampled today by a wet, stampeding moose and no one knows exactly where we are at this exact moment. This is the mess your father has got you into. Just look at us: Bones and blood and skin pulled taut. Flecks of calcium. Breath.

Yet, it is just this kind of vulnerability that attracts me. Each night spent sleeping on the ground is a victory. Each wild sighting, each hawk circling, each stone overturned a welcome retreat from clamor toward curiosity. We get only this handful of chances to rub up against sandstone, to crawl under red willow on our hands and knees, to bury our toes in warm tidal mud.

Stay curious, Rose, despite the odds. Keep your eyes wide open at all times. This is what we are given to love over and over again and to let it go. This tent suits me just fine. There is no real permanence. The only risk is not to come here at all; to never know what it means to be fully alive.

Remember the swans, Rose? That's what I'm talking about.

It was a grey Sunday in February. I don't recall which year, but you were still small enough to hold my hand. It was a season of false springs, when winter had just begun to loosen its grip; when more light appears in the sky, but hardly a time to encounter miracles. Your mother was with us then; we were still a family of three.

Our restlessness took us to Rock Lake, in eastern Washington, one of a string of deep, pothole lakes formed by a series of glacial floods that came pouring out of the Clark Fork, Montana, area during the Pleistocene Era. Geologists say that runoff from the last great flood, 12,000 years ago, reached a height of several thousand feet and moved at more than forty miles an hour across the landscape, sweeping it clean right down to the rock. This beautiful area of scrubbed basaltic canyons and wind-scoured buttes is known, unfortunately, as the "scablands." But it is this type of so-called worthless country that forever attracts me. I've learned to love these scars.

On this day, we trespassed onto private range land. I probably hummed Woody Guthrie's song, "This Land is Your Land," to show my disdain for fencing in the West. You carefully ducked under a barbed-wire fence while I stepped down on the lower strand and lifted the middle one. You crawled through and broke the law for the very first time. I approved.

What were we doing there on a cold, February Sunday, a hundred miles from our Idaho home? What were we searching for? When I think back I believe we were called to this place. You get only so many miracles per life. This was one.

We moved carefully, picking our way around small holes and frozen weeds growing right out of the basalt itself. You were hungry for the lunch we had brought—hot chocolate, egg-salad sandwiches, and fruit. We were hiking uphill, squeezed in the narrow twin tracks of an old cow trail that topped out at the edge of a tiny lake hidden from the road.

You saw them first.

Below us, in an area no bigger than a small suburban yard, rested two hundred trumpeter swans. I thought of white waterlilies with arched stalks submerged below the brackish water, of ice and sky merging. I contemplated the limits of my own movement weighed down by gravity and fear. I knew I was mortal. And I knew that my life would be different from then on.

You immediately sat down and demanded to know the names of the giant ivory birds.

"Trumpeter swans," I whispered, wondering what images those two words brought to your young mind. "They've come a long distance and now they are tired. They mate for life, like wolves."

Then they saw us and began to lift from the water. It seemed to take forever. They rose and circled in a helix, necks straight out, voices low horns sounded in unison, wings stretched to their six-foot limit. They soared over us. We could feel the air from their wings rush across our faces. We laid on our backs and watched them leave.

It was a long time before we ate our lunches. Everything had changed.

Even now, tonight, so far away in years and miles from those swans I am forever lying beneath them, wishing I could go with them, wishing them well.

Rose, I live for such moments now. I live for hope and surprise. I live for swans. That's why I brought you here: so you, too, could find something fleeting to love.

I hear Rose back in the tent stirring. Faint pink streaks appear in the east. Another sleepless night but well worth it. I grab the coffee pot and slip down the path toward the creek for water.

Trumpeter Swans, Rock Lake

Winter evenings I hear the trumpeters
moving over frozen lakes
in the glacial scablands. They are lifting
in a slow, upward helix through holes
in the clouds. They are saying goodbye,
calling reassurance to each other
through falling snow.

Nights like this
I would risk it all for birds.

When the wind is up
I imagine I can still call
the landscape back to earth,
and bury my clean hands
in the warm shallows of tidal mud.
When long wings brush
overhead, when every motion
carries a message of restoration,
I will finally mourn the land.

I believe at birth we are each given
a share of the world's sadness
to carry. No one escapes.
I'm learning to love these swans
because they make a difference.
And I am asking them to hold on too.

Letter to Rose: Visitation

YOU CAME OVER LAST NIGHT with your head lowered. I think you were upset, but when I asked if you were alright you gave back my question with averted eyes. And silence. I will never forget this image: you wore your black, rubber riding boots, the ones from Goodwill. But no gloves, which I didn't discover until next day's school rush. Earlier, as you began the long walk down the driveway to begin this visitation, partially hidden from layers of falling snow, your mother stopped you and whispered some secret that, unwisely, I later quizzed you about.

You are eight years old, but I am asking you to be older.

The lunch pail didn't make it over to this house either, and that night you insisted on making a "sack lunch," as you call it. In the morning, I discover the sack lunch you made the night before consists of six crackers with peanut butter, a handful of raisins, and a banana. Eating is not a priority with either of us. How can we eat with our world upside down?

So many times, in these first scary days of separation, I hold my tongue, wishing you would take the lead and speak, look me in the eye and name the pain we are feeling. Instead, you look away, but you cannot mask the hurt with silence. Not with me. I know you too well. When I try to talk, to somehow be wise, words disintegrate and I am left with the taste of loss and rage. What do you taste?

You were born, my daughter, in the dry, bone-colored ash of Mount St. Helens, washed in the salty foam of the turbid meeting of the Columbia and Pacific at Astoria: our little place of conception.

But that was eight years ago and although I can still find a layer of St. Helens ash in the nearby cedar forests I cannot find an answer to what has happened to our little family. How does hate replace love and why does passion cross back and forth across a thin line between the two?

When I tuck you in, you ask me to close the door so no light penetrates the darkness. This is your custom now. The dark is your refuge. I step outside in the cold to watch the snow take your footprints away, but all I see is you. Over and over again you are walking toward me.

Every Other Weekend

Here in summer's transience of airport terminals,
we pass our offspring back and forth.
And with each exchange they slip
forever into a space
that is neither mother nor father.

Two homes for every child.
More people to love them.
So we say, knowing this is the biggest lie,
knowing children are too flexible for their own good,
knowing we can no longer offer
the protection of two.

Alternating Fridays on my street
goodbyes and adjustments
hang in the air.
Suitcases line the stoops,
the medicines and loaded messages
relayed between unraveled marriages
with enough left unsaid to say it all.
At either home the modest debris of the displaced
stands forgotten: bright Crayons, misplaced
gloves, a form from school "to be signed
by a parent or guardian."

We thought we would get it right
this time, thought we would beat
the matrimonial odds, but this is our legacy.
This is what we create,
these small remains of family,
the ease of letting go.

Pilgrimage

TWENTY YEARS AGO I hitchhiked from Durango, Colorado, where I infrequently attended Ft. Lewis College, to Haight-Ashbury in San Francisco, where a musician buddy lived. In my possession was most of what I owned and certainly all of what I loved: a backpack and sleeping bag. Steel string guitar. Harmonica in the key of C with one of those metal racks that Bob Dylan wore around his neck. A two-year-old blue heeler cow dog named Emmie, who was recovering from kennel cough. Thirty-six dollars. No identification. A journal clogged with songs of imagined heartbreak and poems of intense longing.

March 25, 1975: Dutch-boy haircut. Lady with freckled breasts. Small. Haunting with lonesome eyes. Me. Inside out.

My tattered copy of *On the Road* that fell open to this passage: "Now, Sal," says crazy Dean Moriarty, "we're leaving everything behind us and entering a new and unknown phase of things. All the years and troubles and kicks—and now this! So we can safely think of nothing else and just go on ahead with our faces stuck out like this, you see, and understand the world as, really and genuinely speaking, other Americans haven't done before us. . . ."

My head was full of Dylan, Kerouac, Hermann Hesse, Gary Snyder, and Edward Abbey. My goal was to be a writer, too. I also wanted to be a musician. And an artist. I wanted a girlfriend. I wanted some answers. Now. But what I really needed was seasoning, and like my mentors I turned to the road.

This trip was to be my pilgrimage. Some might call it a middle class white boy's version of a vision quest, but I was sincerely searching for America's heart. I suspected it was somewhere out in the hidden West, out in the landscapes of piñons and mesas, where broad, sweeping shadows fell across desert canyons dripping with pictographs. Places like Nevada's basin and range country. Utah's Canyonlands National Park. Arizona's Oak Creek Canyon (before we loved it to oblivion), and the quirky mining town of Jerome. Where black-eyed vultures hunched up on saguaro cacti waiting for death. Red rock. Rednecks. Bad coffee. Big snakes. Carlos Castanada country.

April 8, 1975: Power lines walk like women holding up their dresses across sage and piñon. The desert screams silent rage. Huge shadows. Mesas, the tabletops of earth.

I craved the same territory where Kerouac and Neil Cassidy careened through in an open-top, chrome-laden '50s Chevy on the way to some noisy jazz joint. I wanted those same smoke-filled, beery hangouts of the beat and hip, and at the end of my road trip I wanted to fall into the arms of a woman who understood everything I ever felt. She would love my three-chord songs and my bad poetry. She would laugh at all my jokes. She would be a non-smoker and thin. (This would actually happen at the age of thirty-eight.)

The Vietnam War had ended. Jimmy Carter was just elected—hell, that alone confirmed anything was possible. I tore up my draft card and tossed it into a Denny's dumpster outside of Grand Junction. I was twenty years old. It was autumn in the West. Screw school.

April 14, 1975: Finals at Ft. Lewis College. It's all I can do to make a showing. I feel so closed in; paranoid about grades. They will not be good grades. But what worries me more is that I just don't care what I get. I just want my freedom back.

It took me six rides, thirty-four hours, and seven bucks to travel the 1,300 miles from Colorado to California. I put my thumb out on a Thursday morning and arrived safely the following Saturday around noon. Coming back a month later took thirteen rides, fifty-eight hours, and nineteen dollars and eighty-eight cents out of the twenty bucks my friend had lent me. (I spent most of that for a night's stay in a motel in Sparks, Nevada, to avoid being jailed for vagrancy.) Single women, elderly couples, and families picked me up. They bought me meals, offered marijuana, told me stories, trusting me with the kind of confessional intimacy usually reserved for spouses and priests. I called it "road energy."

One woman, Benni, even took me home for a cheeseburger in Grand Junction, Colorado. She had jet-black hair like Joan Baez and had been to Belgium. We exchanged addresses. I later wrote her a rambling, passionate letter with Casy's entire soliloquy from *Grapes of Wrath*: "I'm gonna work in the fiel's, in the green fiel's, an' I'm gonna be near to folks. . . . Gonna lay in the grass open 'an honest with anybody that'll have me. Gonna cuss an' swear an' hear the poetry of folks talkin. All that's holy. . . . All them things is the good things."

She never answered. I had imagined lust and attraction, but it was kindness that motivated her. What did I know?

Outside of Reno I met a man and his three-year-old son. He had come down from Sacramento with that month's welfare check and lost every cent gambling. It was only the third day of the month. Now he needed money for a stamp to send an SOS letter to his ex-wife. His son clung to him. They were both hungry. I gave him all the change I had. I never forgot them.

A stonemason working in Colorado picked me up in western Utah. On his way home to Fremont, California, he drank the entire drive, but never appeared drunk. In the middle of the night he stopped at a bar in the small Nevada town of Eureka and told me to wait in the truck. For two hours I watched him through the only lighted window in town, seated at a green, felt-covered table playing poker and drinking shots with men whose faces were shadowed beneath the brims of cowboy hats. I remember it was very cold and I held on to Emmie for warmth. The mason returned in boisterous spirits, buoyed by drink and luck, then drove on through the desert at ninety miles an hour until he swerved off the road into the sagebrush and announced, "crash time," and promptly passed out, using the steering wheel for a pillow. All night I stayed awake listening to coyotes and the sound of a stranger snoring. My life was connected to normalcy by the most tenuous of chances. But that was nothing new.

May 6, 1975: Snow like I can't believe. I just hope my tent pole, which is crooked, does not collapse tonight. I'll try to stay up as late as possible to keep an eye on the tent walls, which are weighed down with wet snow. I'm a bit scared. Everything I own is in this tent and I'd hate to see it ruined. But I will go down with this ship like any loyal captain. Snow is dangerous because it's silent. You can't gauge its intensity or length.

Halfway across Nevada a white government car pulled over. Inside were two army guys in full military dress with crew cuts. They didn't ask where I was going and I didn't ask them their destination. Forty miles later, in the middle of sage and sky, we pulled into Gina's Ranch for Men, one of Nevada's legal brothels, and the only visible structure for miles in any direction. Built like a Hollywood Western set, Gina's had fort-like fencing, a gaudy gate, and plenty of discreet parking out back for the government boys. They dropped me off without a word, leaving me, my guitar, and my dog Emmie standing in front looking (I hoped) out of place. I stood there for hours imagining what went on behind that fence.

One of my last rides, taking me from the mesa red-rock country of southern Utah almost to Colorado, was in a Volkswagon van with Bach on the tape deck and a human anatomy professor from Washington state behind the wheel. Sandstone walls—huge slabs of sliced stones—occupied our attention. Time slowed to match the geology of the place. The professor talked of many things I had no knowledge of, but would in a few years. An ex-wife: "The divorce was her idea. Not mine." His son, who was my age: "He's trying to find himself." The existence of God: "All religions are stupid. When you look at all of this (pointing to crimson cliffs and wrinkled crevices formed twenty million years ago) you realize what endures."

May 13, 1975: I was eating lunch with two seven-year-olds and they got into an argument about tornadoes. So they asked me (a grown-up) to settle their big question: Can a tornado blow down God? I told them no, but I really didn't know for sure. Good question.

Rather than mystical landscapes and jazz clubs, I realize today that what I found instead on my pilgrimage were people straight out of Central Casting for life, each one with a story that would later become my own story. The surprise was not simply the great Western landscape, which continues to engage me as I stumble into my forties. For a few days during a glorious October of golden cottonwoods and unending youth, I discovered a land-scape I had never considered, one that held America's heart and soul. I was not disappointed.

October 30, 1975: My last day in San Francisco. A walk to Chinatown. A patchwork of multi-colored houses with long, wide stairs leading to ornate doors opened by gold knobs. Man playing jazz on an alto saxophone. Old wrinkled wino pulling a box of garbage by a rope. Black kid going down a hill on bike, moving fast, yelling, "No brakes!" A scared woman, shivering in a dark hallway, playing a nylon-stringed guitar, the case open for tips. I gave her a rose.

The professor let me out at a place called Squaw Creek. He was going on to Arches National Park. "I just have a feeling. You know what I mean? I have to be there."

Remainders

WHEN I CALL ROSE at her mother's on this dark winter evening I can hear something wrong in Rose's voice. An emotional quality that a phone cannot disguise. A trouble that needs to escape and come home. She is also irritable and short with me, wanting this conversation to end.

"What's wrong sweetie?" I ask, in a most welcoming tone.

And then suddenly it is freed. "Keith Jensen committed suicide Friday. He tied a rope to his bedroom door and jumped out the window."

Silence. Now we are connected. "School was weird. There are so many rumors. We sat in small groups in Mrs. Spence's English class and tried to talk about it. Some of the kids were crying because the last words they said to him were, 'Shut-up Keith!'

"No one could do any work. I flunked my math test." I look outside the kitchen window at the drifts of heavy snow. I am suddenly shivering, but not from the weather.

I ask Rose if she knew Keith well.

"Everybody knew him. He seemed happy. I never would have thought *he* would do something like this. I don't understand."

She talks on without hesitation, with emotion. I feel as if she is the river and I am the ocean. Then, out of nowhere my daughter says, "Don't worry Papa, I would never do anything like that."

It's a long-standing tradition with us that when we part in person or by phone we each say "I love you." Tonight there is nothing automatic in our goodbyes.

I put down the phone and get out the family album that holds class pictures for each of the last seven years. I find Keith with Rose in C. Anderson's third grade class, and in fourth grade, in Mrs. Strong's class. There is nothing in Keith's face that could forewarn what happened today; nothing to prepare any of us for the idea of a twelve-year-old going to elaborate measures to hang himself. He is smiling out at me along with the other children I have watched over the years: in the noisy playground at Russell Elementary School, on stage at the annual holiday concerts, and at my annual visits on Career Days to talk about writing. These are our children, each and every one a blessing, a gift. Each death affects the entire community.

That's when I remember Keith just for an instant like a light drop of rain. He's at the edges of the classroom on one of the days I visited. I see him looking at me. I recall eyes and a smile. And that is all I remember.

I continue turning the pages of the album and watch the lives of my daughter and me take form. I am driving a tractor raking fall oat straw in northern Michigan; I am balancing baby Rose on the hood of our ancient green truck at a Reno rest-stop; there are April tulips and Rose playing cello; and her mother holding her wrapped in a towel fresh from a bath, both of them radiant.

More pages: Rose with tricycles and summer Popsicles; twirling a dance, eyes closed, in the Palouse wind in a blue corduroy jumper and white tights; she is climbing trees and sniffing North Coast rhododendrons. She walks under the half-light of a redwood forest holding my hand and dances with me, her feet on my own for balance. In every photograph her fingers are busy, her eyes twinkling, and her face reflects the light of each day.

A child's life, with my own intertwined, is held within the covers of this photo album. I can hold each picture and slip into a time frame of emotions. This is what I'm looking for tonight: a reckoning, a validation that the years just didn't pass without notice. The photos are not easy to look at. Memories are never simple. I can't easily untangle the joy from the pain, and if I am to survive separation and divorce, I am forced to choose the better moments of our lives. What fine actors we ultimately become.

All the rooms and houses stare back at me. Meals, friends, seasons, and landscapes of desert and rain. Precious fragments of field and wood. Mountain ranges I still climb at night in my bed. All the various Western towns where I tried to hold us together and failed. I guess these years are finally catching up with me. I think of Leslie Silko's poem *Incantation,*

> "After all bright colors of sunset and leaf
> are added together
> lovers are subtracted
> children multiplied, subtracted, taken away.
>
> The remainder is small enough
> to stay in this room forever
> gray-shadowing restless
> trapped on a gray glass plain."

I close the album. I am haunted tonight. I hear Rose's voice again. *Don't worry Papa, I would never do anything like that.* I am holding still in this room, searching for faith with my own small remainder, affirming one child, remembering another.

Movement Through Corn

We were a captive audience.
Two boys on a train moving
through the heart of the Midwest,
a summer exile to Iowa grandparents.
Our mother, back in Chicago, catching
her breath, our father's whereabouts
unknown, nowhere to be seen,
not outside these dome car windows,
or in the club car
with cigarettes and cards,
not out in the tight green
tasseled alleys of corn,
or in the hills of Dubuque
that rise like bread
over the Mississippi River
where two brothers held their breath,
suspended between air and water,
searching for family
for the benediction
that motion brings.
Eyes pressed flat against the horizon.

Searching for Family in Brooklyn

For one week each summer I travel to Brooklyn from northern Idaho to restore my faith in humanity. I leave behind aromatic cedar forests, wild geese and elegant herons, and the bucolic farming town of wheat where I live, for an attempt at another kind of glory—the glory of family.

I have come to find my father. For three years now I have made the trip to New York to create stories of family while there is still time. I have a daughter now. She needs these stories. We both do.

I look at my life as torn squares of a quilt that needs patching. My entire life has been a search for family. A search for a life preserver to hold on to. Part of the quilt is in Brooklyn. There is something here I need to connect with.

My father and I lost each other over the years for all the wrong reasons: divorce, professional ambitions, and finally, guilt. Our time together is a quiet reconstruction of two lives that went their separate ways. Dad remarried. I endured awkward weekend visits. He moved to New York from Chicago more than twenty-five years ago. I read Kerouac and left for the West at the age of seventeen. Years passed into decades. My mother remarried but I always thought of myself as an orphan. I learned to survive alone. My friends became my family.

I married, then predictably following in the family tradition, divorced, but with a pioneering twist: I didn't walk away. I became a single parent. Rose is my best friend, and together in our single-parent structure we have established our own family traditions. During the summers we explore Montana ghost towns and camp along majestic Western rivers, watching the big sky for red-tail hawks and golden eagles. During the long Idaho winters we hunker down with our books, music, and Hitchcock films. Within these years with Rose lies perhaps the only measure and value of family I have known.

When I was a child and my mother was angry at me she would accuse me of being "just like your father." For years I was embarrassed by everything about my father: his intellect, his stooped walk, and his quietness. Now I realize I am almost exactly like him.

Still there are many blanks and painful moments in my family history. One night in Chicago in a dark room, when I was five years old, my grandmother took turns rocking me and my brother in her arms while the police came and took my father away. Our apartment was flooded in violence. I knew if my grandmother let go of me I would get hurt. The very next memory I recall is a train ride to Iowa to live with her for a year. I always thought my mother was with us, but memories are tricky. Recently a friend asked, "Do you remember if your mother was there at all during that year?" No, I said, suddenly realizing that my history was rearranging itself. Where did she go? I didn't see my father for that entire time, either, and when we came back from Iowa he no longer lived with us and I learned quickly not to ask why.

Now in Brooklyn, we walk the Boardwalk, take a boat trip around Sheepshead Bay, eat dinners in exotic neighborhoods that reek of garlic, visit new relatives that wrap us up in their family quilt without reservation.

With each visit comes a flood of memories and, surprisingly, many of the remembrances involve my father as nurturer: bathing me when I must have been only two; carving animals out of soap bars for my brother and me; watching him bake fudge; his soothing voice at the door when he came home from work. Once all I could say to describe him was, "He's tall. He loves to keep bees."

But my favorite moments are when I have my father to myself. We sit across from each other in the living room—Rose between us—quietly reading as our hearts find a common rhythm. And it is more than enough.

On a bright August morning last summer, a morning when you could believe in Brooklyn, I take a final walk with my father down Oriental Avenue to his subway stop at Brighton Beach. In three short hours Rose and I will be on a plane returning to Idaho, our suitcases stuffed with freshly baked bagels—like exotic riches from the East to hand out to special friends. My father will be in his Manhattan office deciding funding fates for Nobel Prize–caliber scientists. Stride for stride we glide past shopkeepers sweeping their storefront sidewalks, Guatemalan fruit suppliers stocking produce stands, exotic Russian women in babushkas selling gladioli bouquets from shopping carts, and a dozen lyrical languages—none of them English. My father walks tall in an impeccable suit. The avenue parts before us, like we own the place. We are shining in this small part of a great city where these human pockets of miracles still occur.

When my father said his farewell to Rose the previous evening he told her how wonderful she is; not to change anything. She stood in front of him and beamed. We all live for those moments of blessings, when someone sees us with clarity and tenderness. I waited thirty-five years for my father to tell me he was proud of me. Rose doesn't have to wait.

I know how important it is for Rose to periodically leave the West. There is more to life than Idaho can always provide. For example, there's the cheddar cheese omelette and raspberry sorbet Rose had for dinner at the Odeon restaurant in the Tribeca neighborhood of Manhattan. When I asked how her dinner tasted she turned to me and answered with a smile. Rose takes it all in, this huge knot of city, adding images to her young memory.

At the Metropolitan Museum of Art my father buys her a T-shirt and a small, keen book, *The Japanese Fortune Calendar,* by Reiko Chiba. The red cover adorned with Japanese characters and the twelve animals arranged in a circle caught Rose's eye in the lamplight of the museum bookstore. As with all her important decisions and significant pending purchases, she turns the book over and over in her hands, opening the pages bound in blue thread to read the story of the sheep and snake. She puts the book down and walks a short distance away only to return and finally decide.

That entire afternoon took on the quality of a finely bound book. Without meaning to, we create family. It was touching to watch Rose walk with my father through the grand halls of the Met, his hand gently touching her back, guiding her past the dark European paintings into his life.

During another visit to the Met, Rose brings me a book on the history of costume. Who knows what paths this book will trigger? Is this a turning point in her life, finding these brightly illustrated costumes? If I don't purchase this book will it douse a potential career in fashion? Which life will she choose? What will she embrace?

My dimmest reservoirs of recollection are trips upstairs at the age of five or so in our Chicago apartment to play chess with a neighbor and a little bit later picking out melodies on a piano. My mom saying at the time, "I should get him lessons." But we were hopelessly poor and the lessons never came until years later in college in Colorado, during a swarm of isolation and ill-advised wanderings. I haven't played chess since.

What if? What if?

There are so many choices for ourselves and for our children. Anywhere we look there is another door to open. My own goals grow more modest and unattainable with each passing year. I wish for one more night spent outside in the Rockies under trees turning gold and a breeze that picks up with the appearance of the first stars in the eastern horizon. I wish for Rose a life of creativity and meaning. May her hopes stay modest, a reduction back to the basic senses. The poet Czelaw Milosz once wrote, "There was no thing on earth I wanted to possess." The opening of the bedroom window at night and sensing that first gust of evening air; settling down into a calm and hearing the sounds of the street and apartment. Wanting nothing. One clear night without remorse, anger, rage, and guilt. No voices at 2 a.m. Only the twin chestnut trees in the front yard creaking and aging. The sound of my daughter dreaming.

In New York the possibilities are endless and plentiful. All around us are scenarios of the human species. At La Guardia Airport, a woman boards a plane for Nashville. She is crying and disappears into the tunnel sniffling, wiping her nose, glumly handing over her boarding pass. The entire episode takes fifteen seconds, but her sadness—for it is obviously sorrow, not a tearful goodbye—stays with all of us at Gate 3. That's how it is here in New York City: snatches of quick emotions swept up in the swift current of this place of ten million.

A man in Brighton Beach, exasperated with his wife, throws his hands upward toward the sky and screams, "Even the dead you don't like!"

A long, garish Cadillac drifts by ominously with tinted windows, neon license plates, and a bumper sticker that reads, "I want to sex you up."

In Sheepshead Bay, at the El Greco Diner, an elderly woman says, "I'd rather be mugged than go to Alaska." I believe her.

I like the peace my father and I have at the present. Yes, I have questions about the leaving. Someday I hope to get the courage to ask my father what happened; to untangle these dark secrets. "Where did you go?" I want to ask him. "Did you miss me?" I have shadows of childhood terror, memories I don't understand; issues of abandonment that affect my relationships as an adult. But who doesn't? I'm not a victim.

Today, it is enough to sit across from my father over cappuccinos in Sheepshead Bay as he talks about his ability to live a seamless life wherever he is, whether it's "working the bees" in Oneonta, or walking the crowded, steamy streets of Brooklyn. This is what we accomplish each summer. We let the past drain out and the present seep in. What choice is there? We are only given so many opportunities to reach out to each other, to do this work of reconciliation. My father and I deserve what little time is left to indulge in the present and for each to be responsible for his own tricky path through the past.

We say goodbye on the corner of Brighton Beach Avenue. He kisses me. We embrace in the middle of a swirl of passersby, who go around us like we are rocks in a fast Idaho river current. But, for a brief moment, there are only the two of us. I am biting my lip, holding back tears. I thank him, but I don't tell him what for. He doesn't ask. I take in my father, memorize the smell of his warmth, then let go. He climbs the green wooden steps to the Q train, caught in the whirl of humanity, and I watch until he disappears, feeling safe in the most dangerous city in America, a father grateful to be a son at last.

Walking with My Daughter in Brooklyn

Here she will let me hold her hand.
Even at eleven she senses the pregnant woman
begging for dimes and attention, tossing word salad
about the military-industrial complex,
could pull a stiletto or a zip gun
and kill us with as much compunction
as choosing that morning's brand of cereal.
And no one would care.
That's the charm of this place.

Real evil rises above Wall Street
released from manicured hands of the newest caste
of American gentry. It crisscrosses
the Atlantic, the Pacific Rim, makes frequent stops
in Zurich, Berlin, and the Cayman Islands,
this shadowy computerized network.

Here, life and death mean predator and prey.
And neither are winners. Not the cabbie,
the fleet bike messengers, nor the windshield washers
with their greasy rags and rage
who appear from nowhere
when red traffic lights level the odds.
The diamond ring, offered cheap
through the car window by the man
whose quick face you'll never remember,
is so hot it sears temptation
even among the most honest.

I will teach my daughter the word *feral.*
And lessons from these Brooklyn streets:
the way you abandon trust for survival,
the way you get used to the begging
until you turn forever away,
even from yourself.

Eight Days in Brooklyn

MONDAY. "BLACK RAGE. It's a new defense for the Long Island Killer. Sort of like an insanity plea," my dad says, as he drives us toward Brooklyn from La Guardia Airport. Rose and I have just arrived from northern Idaho for our annual one-week visit and we're hungry for news.

Black Rage, he explains, without editorial comment, means that because someone was born black in America and has had to live in a white society that person qualifies for a type of social anguish and hostility. I nod out of politeness. In this case, Colin Ferguson, an African American, is accused of calmly walking down the aisles of a busy Long Island Railroad commuter train and selecting Asian and white victims to shoot. He killed six people and wounded seventeen in the time it takes to pull the trigger a few times on a semi-automatic. Ferguson eventually fired his attorney, William Kunstler, and represented himself. It was a quick trial and conviction.

Since my childhood in Chicago when I routinely rode the "Elevated" downtown, I have always thought of commuter trains as human roulette wheels: you just don't know who is going to enter your car at any given moment and in what particular mental condition they will be. Now we are in New York where everyone is armed and crazy. My neck and back stiffen.

In the back seat of Dad's car I slip Rose a list of emergency phone numbers. "Carry these at all times," I whisper. She stuffs them casually in her shorts and looks at all the graffiti splashed on the freeway viaducts. I wonder if she's experiencing culture shock. I imagine the great blue herons of Idaho lifting their long dark legs quietly as they search for frogs. I am glad they are not here.

"I have to be at work early every day this week," Dad continues, "because an animal rights group, People for the Ethical Treatment of Animals (PETA), is planning to dump a truckload of kitty litter at the front gate of Rockefeller University to protest the use of animals in research."

Dad assures us that Rockefeller only uses rats and mice. No cats or monkeys. Dad is an important higher up. When Rose and I visit him at work we have to be "cleared" at the front gate by a security guard. In New York City money buys you safety. Rose wants to know if they will be dumping *used* kitty litter. I give her one of my fatherly looks.

Tuesday. Robbie—Dad's wife of four years—announces that I should model. "All you have to do is walk into an agency and they'll hire you," she says, looking me up and down. "I'll make some calls."

Robbie has lots of advice. It's her job as columnist for *True Story.* She answers a few letters each month in the magazine and I get to see the rejects. No matter what my mental state is at the time, the letters always cheer me up.

"Dear Dr. Roberta, I'm sixteen years old and planning to marry my boyfriend soon. I love him very much, even though he lies to me and humiliates me. He cheats on me and even carries another girl's picture in his wallet. . . . Do you think we should postpone our wedding?" Engaged, Georgia.

"Dear Engaged: Please don't marry until you both grow up. . . . "
Robbie's previous job was with *The Star.*

Wednesday. The *Times* runs a long piece about the Russian mafia,
which is operating in Brighton Beach, the next neighborhood
over from Manhattan Beach, where Dad lives. The article begins,
"As a Brighton Beach subway train thundered overhead, a hit
man pumped one fatal bullet into the back of Oleg Korataev's
head. It took four rounds in the face and chest to finish off another suspected gangster, Yanik Magasayev. . . ."

All these gangsters have eagle tattoos and their ringleader is
Vyacheslav Kirillovich Ivankov, who is pictured in the photograph wearing a warm-up suit. I don't like his looks.

Most of the Brighton Beach business district is under the
subway platform where the Q and D trains stop. All the signs and
literature —even the menus at places like the Odessa Club and
Cafe Arabat—are in the Cyrillic alphabet. Smells are exotic and
foreign. Stores are packed with exotic breads, eels, fruit, caviar,
gorgeous scarves, sharks, flowers, and great bargains with no sales
tax. Rose buys a school bag for twenty dollars cash. No receipt. I
buy ten packages of rainbow pasta for two bucks.

On Brighton Beach Avenue, two rabbis at a makeshift table
piled high with pamphlets and books stop me. "Do you speak
Russian?" they ask.

"No."

"Are you Jewish?"

When I again answer no they wave me away as if I am a leper.

Every morning at eight, an hour before the banks open,
Russians queue up in front of the doors, standing grimly in line,

not because the banks are crowded, but because it's a habit from waiting for bread and toilet paper in the old Soviet Union.

At the Brighton Beach subway station, someone has crossed out the "CLOSED" sign and scrawled the word "Nyet!"

Thursday. At my dad's university, two PETA members arrive just after noon, wearing gas masks, to dump *used* cat litter at the front gate. They are immediately arrested. Dad set up a room with pastries, coffee, and handouts for the press, but only one radio reporter shows.

Later, Dad shows me some PETA literature that features a cat with electrodes attached to its eyes. The name Rockefeller is prominently displayed. However, the photo is from the University of Oregon, Dad says, and the researcher—whose home number is given—has never used cats in research. Every day he receives death threats.

When Rose and I return to Brooklyn, Robbie, who hates nature, frantically asks me to remove a dead cicada from the walk. Later in the day, she runs over a pigeon and says, "Good, I hit a bird." I scold her and then feel bad. I miss our quiet life in Idaho. I miss birds.

Friday. The *Times* reports the beating death, by neighbors, of a drug addict who attempted to steal ice cream money from a ten-year-old girl. On the news that night is an interview with men who rescued a nine-year-old girl from a sex offender who attempted to drag the girl away from a playground. The sex offender was also beaten but didn't die.

Saturday. Rose, Dad, and I board a small fishing-craft-turned-tour-boat for a Statue of Liberty cruise. I'm not convinced the boat is seaworthy, but I get on anyway, crossing a narrow gang plank to get aboard. Maybe fifty people are on board and we seem to be the only English-speaking group. The Russians lined up an hour ahead of time. The captain is drinking a beer. I doubt it's his first of the evening.

Ten dollars buys a three-hour trip to the Statue of Liberty and back to Sheepshead Bay. All announcements are in Russian. Everyone smokes, drinks Budweiser, and laughs. When Russians get together they know how to live. They will outlive all of us on low fat, high fiber diets. The men are robust, wearing lots of gold and madras. The women are striking. Couples kiss passionately. I'm beginning to feel cheated being from America. I feel plain, unpassionate. I think I see the gangster boss Vyacheslav Kirillovich Ivankov standing on the upper deck looking at Rose and me. I stare at him and try to see if there is an eagle tattoo on his arm. He glares back until I turn away.

Without warning, the loudspeaker blares out Russian rock and roll, perhaps the worst music invented since Wagner. The noise level is disarming. We cruise past Coney Island and the Verrazano Straits into New York Harbor, up the East River, turning at the Brooklyn Bridge, and back out into the harbor. The trip seems to take forever.

The grand finale is the Statue of Liberty where the captain kills the motor just offshore. The statue, remodeled and cleaned up in 1988, is magnificent. We bob and drift in the currents with Ellis Island, dark and mysterious, on our right. Gershwin is playing in my mind, "Rhapsody in Blue," with a single clarinet. Then loudspeakers crackle and the Beach Boys burst out singing

"Barbara Ann." I don't want to think about Brian Wilson in his sandbox at this glorious moment.

In the pitch-black calm families line up for pictures. Flash-bulbs spark and for a second I see the happiness on the faces of these new immigrants. The lights of Manhattan are reflected in all our faces, those who have just arrived and those who were born here. It makes no difference where we are from. America is still the coolest place to be.

Sunday. From the second floor of my father's house in Brooklyn I hear the sounds of the Boardwalk and Coney Island: laughter and music; the lilt of a beautiful tenor voice singing in Russian; children squealing; dogs barking. Languages permeate the humid summer air. The Black Sea Handball Courts are full of serious players, including, I later learn, on-duty ambulance drivers and policemen.

The *Times* reports six homicides in five hours last night. One body was found at 11:40 p.m. under the Verrazano Narrows Bridge, which we passed under on the tour boat at 10:30. I read of a gang rape under the Boardwalk by five men who each took turns putting on condoms so they could not be traced through their semen or contract AIDS from their victim. I begin hiding the *Times* from Rose, but I notice a stack of *True Stories* by her bed with lurid headlines. I am losing control here.

Every five minutes a plane flies over Coney Island trailing a banner: "Cabaret. Tops in Topless. 7 Days." Police helicopters hover just a few feet off the beach. There are no birds anywhere in sight.

I read that New York City averages 5,000 shootings and more than 2,000 murders a year: sixteen and a half shootings and seven murders a day. I'm obsessed with these averages when Rose and I venture out around the city. I picture bullets flying everywhere, searching out warm targets. Rose wants to go to the Gap and buy paisley boxer shorts. I want to stay home and not use up any more chances on the subway. My dad, who rides the subway every day wearing an impeccable suit, carrying a briefcase and a *Wall Street Journal,* says it's just drug dealers shooting other drug dealers.

On the subway I read the month's installment of "Poetry in Motion," an effort by the city to put art in the faces of everyday New Yorkers. "Summer" by Walter Dean Myers: "I like hot days/ sweat is what you get days." Rose reads her book while I assess the mental stability of each new arrival to our car. Each stop nearer to Manhattan feels like a victory. I'm convinced that everyone on the train has a gun or suffers from Black Rage. I warn Rose not to make eye contact. She rolls her eyes.

At McDougal and Bleeker, in the heart of Greenwich Village, we come upon yellow tape isolating a murder scene. A popular jeweler was stabbed to death. The murderer was caught by two unemployed construction workers from Queens, who tackled him as he ran through the streets brandishing a bloody knife. All of this happened just minutes before Rose and I emerged from the subway.

A crowd has gathered outside the jeweler's store, including a man wearing a T-shirt that says, "I'm from New York. I take no shit." This theme of fecal semantics matches the T-shirt in Sheepshead Bay the day before: "Don't ask me for shit."

Monday. Our last day in Brooklyn. Rose and I go to the freak show at Coney Island, where we see the Tattooed Man, who hammers a nail through his tongue; a contortionist, Demonica, who wraps albino pythons around her neck and then bends her body into an impossible box. She also calls herself the Human Octopus. I am asked to tighten a straitjacket around a surly man, who quickly extracts himself from the jacket. I feel as if I'm involved in something pornographic. The same man then lies down on a bed of nails while another audience volunteer stands on top of him. For an extra two dollars we are given the opportunity to watch the pythons feed on live, twelve-pound rabbits for dinner. I think of PETA and decline.

That night at Caroline's Restaurant in Coney Island the dining room is like a scene from a Fellini movie. An organist blasts out the type of schmaltz you only hear at malls, while the diners snap their fingers and sway on every note. Robbie asks the waiter to turn the volume down, but it never happens. All the men wear pinky rings with diamonds. The women are bleached blondes with black eyebrows and purses with gold-plated chain straps. Mirrored walls surround us, magnifying the vastness and surrealism of the place.

Rose orders spaghetti. I consider fish but then remember yesterday's advice in the *Times:* "Due to continued contamination of local waters by PCBs, mercury, and other industrial by-products, the State Health Department suggests that people limit their consumption to one meal (about half a pound) of city-caught fish a week. It also urges women of child-bearing age and children under the age of 15 to avoid the fish altogether, . . ." I had red snapper two days ago.

When the organist plays the first familiar notes of "Happy Birthday," the black-haired Sicilian waiters gather at the table of a large party and sing with more feeling than the small room can hold. Their voices are passionate with an ample amount of vibrato. When they finish, we turn in their direction to applaud, and I catch a glimpse of us in the mirrors. We look like deer caught in headlights.

How We Stay Human

MARY MINERVA MCCROSKEY State Park, balanced high on the edge of Latah County in northern Idaho, is an ideal vantage point to contemplate the value of local Western landscape. At the many viewing areas that bachelor farmer Virgil McCroskey personally bulldozed in the 1940s and 1950s in memory to his mother, you breathe in sweeping vistas of this majestic country.

It's only 4,400 acres balanced on a narrow ridge called Skyline Drive and no one would ever mistake it for wilderness. Logging clearcuts border the park. There is no water; no spotted owls. Towns and wheat fields are plainly visible in the distance. Still, it would be a mistake to dismiss the significance of this park. For it is here that you can see the landmarks by which we measure our lives here in northern Idaho and eastern Washington: Kamiak Butte, Moscow Mountain, Steptoe Butte, Palouse River, and the Palouse hills that ebb and flow like ocean waves. To acknowledge their presence is to begin to know a sense of belonging.

Latah County has never been called a "last best place" in the tradition of dramatic snow-capped peaks, blue-ribbon trout streams, serene lakes, or mystical deserts, but there is a great abundance of natural beauty just beyond one's doorstep.

You need to look a bit harder and stay a bit longer than you would on the banks of Montana's Yellowstone River or Glacier

National Park. But it's easy to love wilderness. I want to love the scars in my own backyard, because that's where my heart is.

These landmarks of forest and field are local anchors of place. And we would be wise in these times of rapid development and boom-town sprawl in the inland West to return often to these places for regular doses of humility and reassembling. I believe it creates a kind of softness in us. For if we forget to look beyond the nonsense and busywork that occupy many of our waking hours, a certain diminishment of spirit takes place.

In Tony Hiss's book, *The Experience of Place,* he quotes a letter from novelist Sherwood Anderson written sometime in the 1920s: "I can remember old fellows in my home town speaking feelingly of an evening spent on the big empty plains. It had taken the shrillness out of them. They had learned the trick of quiet."

For the past ten years I have taken my own shrillness to the forests and fields of the Palouse. I have argued my case to cedar and camas; complained of my own failures to fairy slippers and white pine. Every time I have sought counsel, I have found wisdom and sustenance, and I've become reacquainted with a part of myself that is vulnerable and human. As poet Dixie Partridge writes, "Certain places make a difference/become the wick/that draws out grief/through skin/not diminished/but leavened/into the landscape. . ."

What do we lose each time another tract of land out West falls to a housing development or a super store? In my hometown of Moscow, Idaho, an old barn and house at Sixth Street and Mountain View that was once a part of the outlying countryside is now completely surrounded by swaths of cutouts for the next collection of six-figure-priced homes. "Rolling Meadows Estates." We've already seen what comes next: large box houses—sealed tombs really—tossed across the landscape like giant, clumsy dice. More congestion. More roadside trash. More noise and lights. More strain on city resources. More isolation from neighborhood and community. More of everything *but* "rolling meadows."

In the midst of our current growth spurt of around 3 percent annually, I see more and more prime farmlands and natural areas developed as housing. As the landscape alters from development, that same alteration also changes the very personality of ourselves and our community.

It seemed to happen overnight: wheat fields turned into cul-de-sacs. Rapid losses of landscape create a new type of sorrow. Perhaps we are less able to commit our hearts to loving the land, knowing its fate is uncertain, so easily changeable. If we can't commit to our external landscape of fields and trees, how do we relate to our internal landscape of hearts and minds? And how do we hold on to each other in these times when we need each other the most?

Despite the disruption we will no doubt absorb the new houses and new residents with resignation. We've always been too adaptive for our own good. But will we be able to absorb the loss of trust in the stability of landscape? A new vocabulary is needed. Words that go beyond terms like planning and zoning, in-fill, impacted areas, annexation, and land partitions. We need a way to vocalize a universal loneliness and a sense of displacement unlike any we have known before. And we need to say what it is we are afraid of.

As we hurtle toward change in the West, as the open spaces fill in with new arrivals, we should remind our elected officials and committee members to take into account that there exists among us a vocabulary of the heart, words that perhaps spoke to

Virgil McCroskey when he paused during his labor of love up on Skyline Drive to look south down the valley to acknowledge that the Palouse hills are "inhabited by silent and benevolent spirits." And that on certain perfect Palouse evenings, when the cool air is ripe from the tawny quilt of grain that binds us to this land, one can still hear the forests and fields cautioning us to move slowly, with grace and respect, as if our very lives depended on it.

Cliff Swallows, Hanford Project

And what is the work of a life?
Scars.

It is easy to love the pristine,
the green and glacial. *Wilderness.*
Anyone can possess her. Compliant mistress,
she is won with mere adulation.

Learn to love the scars, the miracles
not of the rainbow, colors
of separation, sorrow, neglect.
Bright glass without fire
is sand. Abandoned desert
highway cracks, retreats to sage
and ravens. Underneath the busiest freeway
hanging swallows nest in mud.
Are you not alone at night?

Lean wild on the edge of nowhere.
Let fear escape over you
until you hear the cries
of coyotes and geese. Don't leave.
Turn, instead, away from yourself.
Notice what holds feather to wing, falcon
to ledge, is a stronger measure of permanence.
Slowly then, these next steps, gracefully,
without a trace back into the grey light.

Drawn to Rivers

SEPTEMBER ARRIVES AND I drive alone through the irrigated fields of the lower Snake River. Onions unravel along the ditches. The air smells of grapes. I can sense the magnetic pull of the river to the north. I am drawn west, to where three rivers converge: the Snake, the Yakima, and the Columbia. A friend tells me that to dam and harness rivers is a patriarchal attempt to control the flow of female energy. It will never work, she says.

Fog raises and lowers its curtain as the elevation shifts. I step into light rain near Kahlotus, Washington, and walk into the brunt of head winds off the Snake ricocheting back and forth up the finger canyons. Wet cliffs lead to sheer drops. I find a train tunnel tucked below the hill, the tracks uprooted long ago. The sound of the wind through the tunnel is deafening. The solitude is intoxicating. Here are the places where I discover how well I know myself. How I am shaping up? I want to keep walking until I reach the river. My daughter keeps me from giving myself completely to the land, crossing the line, and vanishing for good. Instead I crouch in the tunnel away from temptation.

Here is the western boundary of my home territory. To drive much farther than this brings on anxiety. The distance is too far from Rose. Yet, I need to have my fill of new rivers, new birds, and white bluffs like the sentries that guard the Columbia Reach near Richland, the last wild stretch of that great river. I want to climb the Horse Heaven Hills to the summit and wait for the clouds to lift in the west above Mt. Rainier.

I want to fall in love.

And I would bring it all back to Rose as I often have. I can show her the importance of the American bittern I observed at the Burbank Slough near Pasco. Why geese on the wing in September are indicators that there still remains a spirit of wild in the American West. And why five herons flying in formation is a rare event, like Halley's Comet or the Mount St. Helens eruption.

No one taught me these lessons. They were learned on the fly, on weekends, and after ill-timed life changes such as dropping out of school, followed by a string of low-paying jobs. All I ever wanted in my life was to be able to walk and breathe and look around. If I can awaken in Rose a flicker of interest in the immensity of the natural world I will have done my job as a parent.

Each year there is less of the landscape to show to our children. Less mystery. Less sanctuary. Each year our hearts—all of us—leave less space for the unmanaged, the unscheduled, the unimaginable. Maybe bird space is the last refuge of wildness. And maybe, just maybe, the parent-to-child exchange is the final wilderness frontier.

When the first star appears I leave the train tunnel. In the darkness, in the distance, I hear two familiar cries that melt me to the night. Coyote and geese. I am home.

Our New Neighbors

A NEW COUPLE moved into the apartment next door in this ancient Idaho Victorian. They are using the same bed as the previous couple, Nicole and Peter, whose lovemaking I could hear quite dramatically when their headboard pounded my living room wall. Sometimes I could hear Nicole moaning and I felt comforted, although it was always hard to face them in the lobby after one of their interludes.

Their replacements—newlyweds—moved into Apartment One without any furniture or boxes or luggage. Both of them are smokers with loud barroom voices and heavy footsteps. The woman is a blond, maybe twenty-three; the man wears an old army jacket and his age and hair color are indistinguishable. He seems affected. When he says hello he talks much too loud as if there are other people around that only he can see.

One balmy evening in February as I watched the waxwings come in to feed I saw the man in the backyard with a metal detector, waving it back and forth like a scythe or a mine sweeper. He had a cigarette dangling from his lips and completely ignored his wife, who twirled by herself in a revealing sun dress that exposed her white back and long thighs. I predict they will fight passionately until the lines of their marriage are drawn so they can survive the future together.

My daughter Rose and I have lived in this house for five years. We are the tenured residents and we have our routines. Rose falls asleep to her AM station on the clock radio I gave to her for her thirteenth birthday. She loves the song "Five Hundred Miles," the hit from the movie *Benny and Joon*. My bedroom shares a wall with Apartment One's bathroom. They have a shower. We don't. Our cold water faucet handle falls off when the bath is running and we have an infestation of carpenter ants and ladybugs. Rose is almost six feet and will need a new bed soon. She likes the fan kept on in her room all night, even in the winter. I stay up until dawn making lists. And listening.

Our neighbors always move out after about six months for better standards of living. When Nicole and Peter left I found a snotty handwritten note in my mailbox concerning my attitude toward Bunny, our calico Manx, whom I really don't care for. The note ended, "Have fun in Chang's slums." Mrs. Chang is our Chinese landlady, who lets me pay the rent late and rarely does any maintenance on the house or the thirty others she owns in town.

We are quite poor. We have no savings and my checking account is one big historical overdraft. Sometimes for dinner I make popcorn laced with brewer's yeast and soy sauce, and I swear it tastes like steak. I think of coffee as food. I spent my last two dollars at the new espresso cart.

I hope I don't smell the cigarette smoke from Apartment One. I hope they make love a lot and that their fights don't involve hitting each other. The new woman is quite striking. The man—like most men—intimidates me with his violent voice and metal detector. Both of them stomp across the old wood floors like characters from "The Invasion of the Body Snatchers."

I ran into Nicole at the Moscow Food Coop. I was visibly cool. She was surprised to see me. She probably had no idea how small a Western town is; that snooty notes concerning the treatment of cats eventually come around in aisles of instant split pea and bins of organic menstrual sponges. I wanted to tell her that despite the ants and ladybugs I am not raising my daughter in a slum; that home is what you make it, that humility comes with age and sometimes wisdom never arrives. I wanted to tell her that their lovemaking sessions were shorter than average. Instead, I said nothing, saving the above soliloquy for the drive home.

I want to take Bunny for a long ride in the country and dump her in a wheat field and drive off in a cloud of gravel. But I'm terrified of picking her up and she's only ridden in a car once.

If I ever date again it will be with one of those idealistic twenty-year-olds at the Coop who never shave or wear foundation garments; who tie their long hair in scarves and talk to everyone like they're an old lover they had parted with because one of them got a job at the Farm in Tennessee. I look at them and think in this order: big hair, breasts, arms, bracelets, ankles, smiles, Sufi dancing, gardens, tea, children, breasts, Central America, new age, space, heartbreak.

The new neighbors—the woman's name is Rita—have lived here a week now and I don't think they've made love yet.

My therapist suggests I volunteer my time at the Coop. I could meet someone *and* get the 18 percent member discount. When the phone rings after 10 p.m. I get frightened and my heart beats abnormally. The answering machine is on all the time, but no one ever calls.

I asked Rose this summer when we were camping in Montana if she knew how scared I get sometimes. She shrugged and said she didn't notice anything particularly strange.

Within the Heart
of a Landscape

Here are guideposts
to my seasons: Yarrow.
Mullen. Shooting stars.
Paintbrush. Cornflower.
Blue bells. Mule ears.

Living inside the heart that's
what I'm after—dry
bunchgrass just before
the stillness and the thunder,
the world within the world.

The Eagles of Beauty Bay

TEN BALD EAGLES, resembling giant black and white kites, cast themselves back and forth in the updrafts between Beauty Bay and Mineral Ridge in an eastern inlet of Lake Coeur d'Alene. Their seven-foot wingspans never waver from steady flight and their ivory heads—more precisely, their yellow eyes, which see eight times sharper than our own—notice every move we make from the road.

Tamarack and grand fir comb the mist that hovers over the bay. It's mid-afternoon and the eagles are through feeding on the dying kokanee. The eagles will slowly circle back to their favorite roosting trees, dropping the half-eaten carcasses of the lake salmon to the forest floor where giant, scavenging ravens continue the biological balancing act while beetles and ants wait their turn in the food chain. When the salmon are depleted the eagles will turn their attention to thinning out old or sick ducks. Easy pickings. Not surprisingly, no ducks are to be seen. On the lake the word is out: The eagles are back.

No need for the Audubon bird guide today. We can easily look across the small bay and identify five eagles roosting in a tree. We look for white heads, white tail feathers, and a regal, somehow patriotic attitude we foolishly attach to them. For eagles care nothing about our red, white, black, and blue attitudes. Our pomp and dire circumstances. They are hungry. That's all.

Kokanee in the lake live four years then come back here to spawn and die. I can only speculate but I think the fish know exactly what they need to do every day of their 1,400-day life cycle. How I envy them.

We have driven more than three hours on this low-light, overcast day in late December through the lake country of northern Idaho to see the annual bald eagle migration. We brought peanut butter and raisin sandwiches on freshly baked sourdough bread; small carrots that snap in our mouths like dry willow; a thermos of cocoa; and large slices of walnut-pumpkin cake dusted with powdered sugar that falls with each bite like sticky snow onto our sweaters. This is food to be eaten outdoors.

We are not alone. Car after car pulls into a nearby campground and families get out and walk leisurely along the road—binoculars and children in tow. From the looks of clothing, age, and make of cars (or "rigs" as Westerners call any combustible engine vehicle), the entire social strata is here. Logger and lawyer. Masseuse and machinist. Farmer and flight attendant. Judging by the smiles and conversation, there seems to be complete consensus. Finally. Today, everyone in northern Idaho is pro-eagle.

How could we not love these eagles? If we cannot love these birds we cannot love anything. If we forget to connect their lives of wildness to our own we are ultimately lost. Perhaps it's too late on a large scale to teach an interest and respect for the natural world. But on a one-to-one, father-to-daughter scale, anything remains possible. I have lived with the proof for fourteen years and she stands beside me today.

Rose is less interested in the eagles than she would have been a couple of years ago. Separation is not far off and her own identity is emerging, an identity that may not include bird watching or hiking through the icy wind of Lake Coeur d'Alene. I know she'd rather be with her friends than with parents and bald eagles, listening to the rock band Counting Crows instead of counting eagles with Dad. Still, there is something here she will take away from this afternoon although she does not know that yet. Someday, no matter where she is, she will remember birds, pine trees, December light; the distinctive musty odor of ancient lakes, the narrow roads that wind past the living rooms and kitchens in the hard-nosed, blue-collar Idaho timber towns like Harrison and Emida, where the order of each and every day is an unglamorous form of gritty survival.

If, up to this point, I have done my parenting job well she might recall these reference points of landscape and maybe realize her own place in this green world of canyons, five-fingered ferns, river rocks, forest canopy, and eagles. The memory of this particular day might surface in a dream or arrive in the form of a certain slant of light, the scent of pine tree, a spoken word, a photograph, the texture of a piece of clothing, or a passage from a book.

My parenting is in a new, unenviable stage. During these teenage years I see myself in a struggle for the very soul of my daughter. Her attention is elsewhere as she searches for her own ideals. Age-old values found in nature and the hearth of home; the celebration of the humbly ordinary are mocked and opposed by the noise of our billion-dollar image industry that promotes ridicule, accumulation, promiscuity, and transience. How can a parent's voice emerge through the constant barrage of flashy, digital images perfectly choreographed to rock and roll and rap? How do I compete with a de-evolving culture that promotes passive attention and loneliness, but never a serious emotional commitment? Nature and the biological kingdom have few advocates. It's up to me to promote this world to Rose.

Reliable role models of parents, grandparents, community and religious leaders (the honest ones), and teachers, have been co-opted by the empty sound bites of illiterate athletes, spaced-out "musicians," and millionaire actors with impeccable bridge-work. Overnight success without hard work is the message of the day in the videos, ads, and movies that assault my daughter. The one overriding question in American culture remains: "What's it like to be rich and famous and beautiful?"

How conservative I must seem to Rose. Papa with his field guides, maps, binoculars, acoustic music, who, at the drop of a word can rant and rave on every subject from beer commercials and karaoke to lotteries and militias. During one struggle, I suggest canoeing. She makes a face. Let's go look at flowers on Kamiak? She tells me I'm old. Her bedroom door closes. When I open it a poster of rock musician Courtney Love glares down at me with the words, "Live through this." Sometimes, late at night I hear her push the plastic buttons on her Walkman (the worst contraption ever invented), followed by the industrial buzz of Nirvana, Hole, and Green Day. Recently, she proudly quoted a friend, "Nature is boring. Nothing happens." Exactly my point.

Humility. That's one quality I'm trying to teach Rose today in this icy corner of Idaho. The idea is to show her an alternative to this media madness and lonely egotism, a place where she can hear her own internal message. Rose will eventually struggle through the noisy clamor of this culture, the coming of age, and draw her own conclusions about the worth of both worlds.

Have I adequately prepared her for life's fights? I review my mental list of axioms. The final list of fatherly advice: clip coupons and always buy generic. Memorize some lines of poetry. Learn to play a musical instrument. Exercise, but never weigh yourself. Make a lot of money and then give it all away. Learn the names of flowers, plants, and birds. Sleep with the windows open. Recycle. Eat out only in small town cafes where the waitress is also the cook, bartender, and day care coordinator. Volunteer in the community. Cultivate solitude. Forgive yourself. Bring your own bag to the grocery store. Never date a man that sports a National Rifle Association sticker on his rig. Don't run the water needlessly when brushing your teeth. Use less of everything. Hug a tree. Don't spit. Be of good cheer.

I sneak a look at my daughter. Behind her five foot, eleven inch, frame I see the eagles circling, creating a halo above her. She has certainly come a long way since those early days full of fear more than five years ago. She is an outgoing ninth grader, surrounded by life-long friends—her support group. No longer immersed in full-time introspection, Rose plays volleyball and sings in the alto section of the Moscow Junior High Select Choir. At a recent volleyball game, her mother, also sitting in the bleachers watching Rose run around the court full of confidence, screaming encouragement at teammates, turned to me and said with astonishment, "She's normal!"

I think of our first trip after divorce unraveled our family, and how hard it was just to get out of bed each morning and make coffee. In our search for a new place in the world we trusted in the feeling that comes from trumpeter swans in flight and the sudden burst of an antelope across our path. The less dramatic was equally important; simple tasks of putting up a tent, sitting on river rocks, hiking, boiling water, and taking the time to identify hawks, songbirds, and the mica-encrusted shelters of the caddisfly. For a while we stopped talking. And with all our collected might, we ran until all we could hear was wind in our ears. Now we have stopped running.

We began to name the world around us. In the white pine forest north of Moscow we came across the ghostly brown parasitic Indian pipe flower, devoid of chlorophyll and leaves, that gathers nutrients from nearby green plants. We learn of its family, wintergreen, with familial connections to pinedrops and candysticks. On the northeastern slope of Kamiak Butte, in early spring, grows the fairy slipper, or calypso, of the orchid family, which was named, according to Audubon's *Field Guide to North American Wildflowers,* "for the sea nymph Calypso of Homer's *Odyssey,* who detained the willing Odysseus on his return from Troy; like Calypso, the plant is beautiful and prefers secluded haunts." Indeed, the fairy slipper is a skittish orchid that hides under ferns in the moist parts of the forest.

Fairy slipper leads to another thought, a connection to the opposite of the flower spectrum, the gaudy Indian paintbrush, a member of the figwort or snapdragon family and a partial parasite, with relatives like the monkeyflower and purple Chinese houses. Not shy at all, paintbrush prefers open, exposed slopes, where it shows off its fireworks of colors in reds and oranges.

Preferences. Personalities. Temperaments that run the gamut. Like all families.

Maybe these discoveries have to do with focus and awe, that our own problems can be overshadowed by simply stepping outside and paying close attention. We gather strength from a world that demonstrates power in forms that make our crude efforts puny in comparison. And at the time Rose and I were unconnected to family, landscape took us in.

I've undergone my own changes. On one of the only days in October when the clouds broke I married Jan. Again the landscape played a critical part. We courted and sparked on this gentle, rolling Palouse carpet of wheat; out on the soft, tawny fabric of grain that hides a distinctive, sensual cereal smell that fills all the houses in northern Idaho and eastern Washington in August, reminding us year after year there is more here than espresso, pizza, and universities. There is also agriculture, that enduring work of sowing and harvest. This is what drew us in to each other in those first brilliant months.

All spring and into our first summer, on our trips out on the wheat, Jan taught me about light; how the Palouse hills take on a certain texture of color just before dusk, as if the hills release the day's light back into the sky. Dark green against cobalt before a storm. Ocean blue on calm days, a backdrop for the high-low, two-note song of the black-capped chickadee. She taught me to look closely at the "eyebrow places," curved swatches of undeveloped farm land on the sides of hills, remnants of the old Palouse prairie that hide pheasants, camas, quail, long-eared owls, and blue-eyed grass. "Those are special places," she said, stars and sparkles filling her brown eyes. I had never noticed them.

Now in our home we watch house finches and white-crowned sparrows that find their way to the birdbath. We marvel at the endurance of the natural world. Twice a day, during the warm months, we take garden tours around the yard, watching the feathery blue flax bloom, and the sphinx moths stick their long tongues down into the coral bells, and we measure the daily progress of the ribbon grass Jan brought back on the plane from her beloved Illinois prairie where she was raised.

Jan and Rose already share the banter and sisterhood of women. I can see the two of them becoming allies, and I will have to step out of the way. I am outnumbered. I am a lucky man.

At the wedding I read these words to Rose: "The last five years, when it's been just the two of us, have been precious and I'll always have a special place in my heart for those years. There is little we haven't shared. Afternoon trips to the swimming hole followed by milk shakes in Kendrick; our camping trips to Yellowstone, climbing the steep trail to the Madison Buffalo Jump, the evening we saw the knot of white western pelicans in the drizzle, the unusual cloud formations over Philipsburg, the antelope range at Hart Mountain, our bird watching weekend at Malheur, exploring ghost towns in Montana. Steens Mountain. Volleyball in the yard. Our quiet dinners. I love your curiosity and insights. At times the lines have been blurred as to who is teaching whom.

And I've admired your kindness, your character, your poise and beauty. At fourteen you possess a wisdom that I certainly didn't have at that same age, and I'm not sure I have it yet. All fathers should be so lucky to have such a daughter. I am so proud of you. Thank you Rose, not just for the last five years, but for all the years we shared, and for accepting Jan into your life. "

Divorce and loss has brought us a special form of closeness we might not have ever attained otherwise. It also brought us a type of emotional street smarts. Poet Tess Gallagher describes it best as a "refugee mentality . . . you learn to be industrious toward the prospect of love and shelter. You know both are fragile and that stability must lie with you or it is nowhere. You make a home of yourself." Broken family? At first. But not now. Stronger? Definitely. Wiser? Rose is. Whether I am is open for lively debate.

Sundays Rose returns to her mother and stepfather. I am never prepared. It is always an awkward emotional transition to have your child for one week, then lose her for the next. To never know how dramatic to make your goodbye. Sometimes before she leaves, bags of clothes and a tangle of shoes, books, and tapes stacked up at the door, we play volleyball in the back yard. Over and over again I serve hard line drives to her and she gracefully returns the serves with artful digs. With each return of serve the heaviness lifts as the physical activity overtakes the mental gymnastics of assessing this court-mandated separation.

Then we load up the car and drive to her mother and stepfather's house in Deary. It's a route that takes us through the best of this Palouse country. East from Moscow, fields give way to patches of tamarack and fir, with the occasional aspen grove and the cul-de-sacs of new California ranch-style housing. Along the way, Paradise Ridge, Tomer Butte, and Buffalo Hump rise to the south; the wheat, dry pea, and rapeseed fields are in various stages of ebb and flow and color combinations, as are the many varieties of flowers and plants, such as wild roses, lupine, and yellow peas. At Joel, a mere trace cluster of houses and trailers, a silver grain elevator is the tallest structure around. The road curves sharply, and to the north are beautiful panoramic views of Moscow Mountain, with its smaller twin towers descending off the Palouse range to the west and eastern Washington.

After passing Carlson's orchard and used car lot, a rush of cold air hits us no matter what time of year and we descend Driscoll Ridge, past Clint's auction business and antique shop on the right, situated in a dark, northern exposure where the last patches of the previous winter's snow can be found. Then the smell of cedar from the mill yard, the combination minimart-laundromat-car wash ("Power Ball, 30 Million, lattes .99¢, Smoky Joe sale"), the wide main street of Troy, usually littered with logging slash, the new library and post office, the general store where locals can still buy groceries on a tab, the Troy Phone Company, the Troy Tavern, the ubiquitous video store operating out of a converted gas station, then a sharp turn east out of town across the rarely used Burlington Northern Railroad tracks. This drive through town takes two minutes.

On the other side of Troy the country gets steeper and the croplands give way to larger stretches of forest land, with ponds and marshes. The sky opens up. We share the road with chip trucks, grain trucks, horse trailers, skunks and badgers, shiny shards of mica, belching pickups with gun racks loaded with firewood from the Clearwater National Forest, road graders, road kills, deer, boats, kestrels and northern harriers, and house trailers. Green signs appear in front of homesteads: "This family supported by timber dollars." We pass the Spring Valley turnoff, two gravel pits, and dirt roads that lead to three clay pits. There's the Troy and Deary Gun Club, Zimmerman's Logging with the gigantic wooden logger carving in front of the office, then front yards full of pinto horses and automobile husks, ragged outbuildings, and red barns. We dip down Dry Ridge, over the seasonal Bear Creek, and up again past the small sign leading to Zion Cemetery. ("A good one," Rose says, looking out the window. She should know. She's been to every one of them in the county.) Finally, after twenty-six miles, Potato Hill—Spud Hill to everyone in northern Idaho—leans into view, and we shift down, passing the Deary sewage pond, the Washington, Idaho and Montana Railroad tracks, to Rose's country home just off the highway.

We say our goodbyes in the yard—my well-practiced lines: "Call me this week, OK?" I find Rose's eyes, then hug, and we go our separate ways. Driving back to Moscow, I think, "This makes absolutely no sense at all." It's just one of many self-defeating thoughts that I'll spend the next six days digesting.

After I return home, I often look for solace in the form of a photograph on my desk of Rose from one of our camping trips. Within the silver frame, she stands on a tumble of giant, lichen-splashed rocks on the shore of the Selway River. Moving up the valley behind her is an early summer shower, the kind of weather Rose was born in and still thrives in. Her long hair rises as the barometer drops; arms crossed, long fingers relaxed. Her dark eyes stare back, unwavering. Her mouth is closed, set in the slightest of smiles. Her age is hard to guess. If you came across this girl you would immediately take a step back. You would tell her only the truth. You would hear the distant thunder rumbling somewhere over the craggy peaks of the Bitterroots and associate her forever with ancient river rocks and gathering clouds of electricity. And strength.

She looks back at you. Unblinking. Determined. She is saying, to all of us, I am ready for anything.

Acknowledgments

MANY LANDSCAPES AND PEOPLE have found their way into my heart. I have not forgotten where I came from.

Thanks to my grandfather, Charles Uchytil, for taking me fishing and for all the great trips in his pickup truck to the family farm in Iowa; blessings to my late grandmother Georgia for keeping me in line—you are missed but not forgotten. My brother David offers inspiration by his high standards of compassion and generosity. I owe a tremendous debt to my mother Charlene for her guidance in the face of so many obstacles.

My Brooklyn family includes my father, David, who is open to all my manifestations, and a joy to be with, whether we are picking apples in eastern Washington or negotiating the subways of Manhattan. Robbie Temes has been my advocate from the day we met, and I look forward to our next morning with *The Times,* bagels, and gossip.

My deep appreciation to my family in Durango, Colorado: Joe Fowler for first showing me the beauty of the natural world and for all our adventures around the Southwest, when there was no money, only landscape; to Rita Fowler for her wisdom, friendship, and fierce love of her native state; to Jeanne Fowler for all the encouragement and literary conversations; to Ellen Benson, who is a natural born writer if there ever was one; and to Barbara

McGuiness, who shares our history at Lemon Dam. Also, warm memories of Emmie Lou and all the hikes up Miller Creek.

Brock Mehler taught me the magic of storytelling through music with guitars and coffee during those endless afternoons in Animas Valley watching the narrow gauge train come down the San Juan Mountains from Silverton. Thanks for all those highway songs.

My Palouse family includes John Black and Kathleen Anspach, who have both been with me through the best and the worst of times, and have not run away. The same goes for Warren and Beth Case and Cindy Johnson who have also shared my joys and failures.

Keith Petersen at WSU Press made this book a reality, injecting clarity and vision to the pages. Jo Savage added the beauty of design. Beth DeWeese and Mary Read were early manuscript readers and steadfast supporters.

Finally, I want to acknowledge my wife, Jan Ellen Engel Gantz, who shows me all the different ways to look at landscape and life, while making our home a safe haven of books and music. I am looking forward to all our tender days to come out on the wheat.

Stephen J. Lyons
Pullman, Washington
June 1996

About the Author

Since coming West twenty years ago, Stephen J. Lyons has been employed in six different states as a tree planter, daffodil picker, dude ranch cook, ice cream vendor, magazine editor, newspaper reporter, tofu maker, grain truck driver, assistant dairy herdsman, and agricultural extension editor. He once worked for a week in Colorado pulling nails out of boards, and for one twelve-hour day picking hops in southern Oregon. (He was fired from the hops job after accusing the foreman of having bad karma.)

He is a product of the Chicago public school system, and attended both Ft. Lewis College and the University of Idaho. Lyons's poems, essays, and articles have appeared in many publications, including *The Detroit Free Press Sunday Magazine, Witness, The Saturday Evening Post, Utne Reader, The Chronicle of Higher Education, Northern Lights, Idaho's Poetry, High Country News, The Sun,* and *Manoa*. He lives in Pullman, Washington, and works in Moscow, Idaho.